PRAISE FOR *BELO*

"*Beloved Dust* is an intelligent vision for life with God through prayer, and many of its rich images have stayed with me long after I put down the book."

--SHAUNA NIEQUIST, AUTHOR OF *Bread & Wine*

"In *Beloved Dust*, Kyle and Jamin tell us the truth about who we are and why we're here in a way that will draw you closer to God. Here is great wisdom on spiritual growth and friendship with God; written by two people whose friendship for each other is evident—and who will become your friends before the end of the book."

--JOHN ORTBERG, AUTHOR OF *Soul Keeping*

"*Beloved Dust* is an important look at the most important aspect of life—what a genuine relationship with God really looks like. Jamin Goggin and Kyle Strobel address our expectations and frustrations about spiritual growth in a hopeful, empowering way. *Beloved Dust* strikes the rare balance of being rich and deep while remaining practical and engaging. This book delivers on what it means, and doesn't mean, to grow in a relationship with God."

--JUD WILHITE, AUTHOR OF *Pursued*; SENIOR PASTOR OF CENTRAL CHRISTIAN CHURCH

"In a culture of pop Christianity that serves a fast food gospel for consumers wanting drive-by spirituality, Goggin and Strobel defy expectations. Their book leads the reader on a slow, inward journey to discover the deeper hunger in their souls--a hunger for God himself. It is a beautiful and gracious exploration of prayer that everyone seeking a truer, deeper, and more authentic life with Christ should read. This book will draw you into a richer communion with God as it did for me, and that is the highest compliment I can possibly offer."

--SKYE JETHANI, AUTHOR OF *With* AND *Futureville*

"The book in your hands will remind you to stop, to revel in God's fatherly presence, and to just *be*--that God is God and you are you; that you are his; and that our dustiness is a beautiful thing. I am thankful for Jamin and Kyle's gift to us within these pages."

--TSH OXENREIDER, AUTHOR OF *Notes From a Blue Bike*

BELOVED
DUST//

BELOVED DUST //

DRAWING CLOSE TO GOD BY DISCOVERING
THE TRUTH ABOUT YOURSELF

JAMIN GOGGIN
AND KYLE STROBEL

NELSON
BOOKS

An Imprint of Thomas Nelson

© 2014 by Kyle Strobel and Jamin Goggin

All rights reserved. No portion of this book may be reproduced, stored in a retrieval system, or transmitted in any form or by any means— electronic, mechanical, photocopy, recording, scanning, or other—except for brief quotations in critical reviews or articles, without the prior written permission of the publisher.

Published in Nashville, Tennessee, by Nelson Books, an imprint of Thomas Nelson. Nelson Books and Thomas Nelson are registered trademarks of HarperCollins Christian Publishing, Inc.

Published in association with literary agent Jenni Burke of D.C. Jacobson & Associates, LLC, an Author Management Company, www.dcjacobson.com.

Thomas Nelson, Inc., titles may be purchased in bulk for educational, business, fund-raising, or sales promotional use. For information, please e-mail SpecialMarkets@ThomasNelson.com.

Unless otherwise noted, Scripture quotations are taken from THE ENGLISH STANDARD VERSION. © 2001 by Crossway Bibles, a division of Good News Publishers.

ISBN-13: 9780529110206

Library of Congress Control Number: 2014937731

Printed in the United States of America

14 15 16 17 18 RRD 6 5 4 3 2 1

We dedicate this book to our children. You were in our hearts as we wrote. We are humbled and honored to be called by God to father you, and we pray that our lives will be a model of what life with God can look like. More importantly, we trust that the Lord will call you into his life and that you will follow him in his way of love. We love you, delight in you, and hope deeply that you will know the ceaseless love of God.

Kyle's Children:

To Brighton: You are strong, passionate, and inquisitive. I pray that these gifts become opportunities to be with the Lord in all things, knowing his strength and calling for you.

To Oliver: You are strong, sensitive, and so full of joy. I pray that these gifts will allow you to rest in the Lord and know his sensitivity, strength, and joy for you.

Jamin's Children:

To Emersyn: You are loving, compassionate, and wise. I pray that God will use these gifts to teach you his love, compassion, and wisdom in the depths of your heart.

To Sawyer: You are creative, tenderhearted, and courageous. I pray that these gifts will be used by the Holy Spirit to invite you into the unique adventure he has charted for your life.

To Finnley: You are joyful, inquisitive, and strong. I pray that these gifts will allow you to abide in the Lord and to know his strong love for you.

> *I have you fast in my fortress,*
> *And will not let you depart,*
> *But put you down into the dungeon*
> *In the round-tower of my heart.*
> *And there will I keep you forever,*
> *Yes, forever and a day,*
> *Till the walls shall crumble to ruin,*
> *And moulder in dust away!*
> —HENRY WADSWORTH LONGFELLOW

CONTENTS //

FOREWORD //

AS PASTOR OF Saddleback Church for the past thirty-three years, I have walked with people through every facet of their lives with God. What I have learned is that devout followers of Jesus often struggle to grasp an abiding relationship with God. What does it mean to grow in this relationship? What does it look like to follow Jesus in one's day-to-day life? This is what people are hungry for.

I can hardly think of two people better equipped to explore these realities than Jamin and Kyle. I have known Jamin and Kyle for many years and have watched as they've matured in the faith. Through their years of study and ministry, they have developed an uncommon depth of wisdom. It is out of their personal journeys, their studies, and their ministry experiences that they present a compelling and powerful vision of the Christian life. They have something to say that needs to be heard.

In this book you will encounter a vision of the Christian

life that is biblically grounded and life applicable. Jamin and Kyle take you on a journey through the story of God's redemption to paint a powerful picture of God's calling for your life. If you are wondering what it really looks like to grow in your relationship with God, you will find it here. If you find yourself burned out and fatigued by trying to work hard at Christianity, you will discover an invitation to rest and refresh your soul in God. If you are wondering how your faith should inform your everyday life, Jamin and Kyle provide clear and sound answers. If you find that your prayer life has hit a rut, or you are struggling to really connect with God, Jamin and Kyle give you a way forward. They argue that the heart of Christianity is to be with the God who is always with us. We are called to practice the presence of God at all times and in all places, and therefore we must learn what it means to abide in his love.

Jamin and Kyle explore all the questions and challenges that face us as we seek to grow in relationship with God. Rather than avoiding the deep issues of our faith, they face them head-on. In this sense, the book before you is bold and courageous. The authors want to wrestle with the questions of your heart and treat them with the dignity they deserve. They don't avoid the parts of faith that often confuse or frustrate us. Rather, they address them directly. This is why I love this book so much. It is not a surface-level study of life with God, but rather deeply explores all the twists and turns of our lives as Christians.

This book cannot be treated lightly, because it is a book that offers a weighty promise. Jamin and Kyle are committed to offering you the life God has for you. A life of beauty and abundance. A life of love and joy. A life with God-shaped purpose and meaning. This is the life God has for you. This is the life I want for you. That is why I believe this book is so important.

What you will find in these pages is the very heart of the matter. Nothing could be more important than discovering what it means to love the God who loves you. So, let me speak as a pastor: please read this book. Read it slowly and prayerfully. Read it with an open mind and an open heart. Read it and discover the life God truly has for you. You will not be disappointed!

—Rick Warren

INTRODUCTION //

AS THE ROOM began to fill, I (Jamin) became aware of the myriad of expectations before me. Each person in the diverse group had sacrificed time and money to go on a spiritual retreat that I was leading. Consciously or unconsciously, every person in the room was longing for something.

What I have found over the years is that most of the expectations boil down to one of two things. People go on retreat to either fix something or experience something. Often it is both.

"Just tell me what I need to do to fix my spiritual life."

"I just want to feel God's presence in a powerful way."

Though most of us can relate to these inclinations, they are misguided. Guiding people into what God truly has for them often involves tearing down these expectations. This requires grace and discernment. They must lay down their expectations and open their hearts to whatever it is God has for them on retreat. It is hard to receive a surprise gift with appreciation and joy if we have preconceived notions about what the gift will be.

We are more often than not going to be let down. Likewise, if I do not help dismantle these expectations right from the start, they are likely to result in trouble. "This isn't what I thought I was going to get." "This is all there is?" The gift they do receive is disappointing and maybe even discouraging.

Whereas I am a pastor, and Kyle is a professor, we often encounter similar shepherding opportunities. When we meet up with parishioners or students, we often hear the same expectations and struggles. They desire something from God that they are not getting. They may be scared to admit it, but the truth is the Christian life sometimes feels frustrating and empty. They were told, "Christianity is about a relationship, not a religion of dos and don'ts." Indeed, many of them have said these very words countless times, but they now feel hollow. Like a company slogan you have been trained to use when encountering first-time customers, this cliché once touched something true about your experience that is now far from clear in your heart. What does relationship with God really look like?

In Christ, God has called us to be with him. He has invited us into relationship. He wants us. But do we want to be with God? Do we truly want him? Unfortunately, as we have just seen, the truth is we often want a sense of control and accomplishment rather than God. We want an experience rather than God. In the midst of this, the real issue of the heart has been exposed: we want to form God in our image rather than be formed in his. Instead of embracing him, we turn to ways to control and create meaning on our own terms. This leads to an inner dialogue that focuses on ways to fix ourselves rather than ways to be with God:

"If only I could be more diligent about practicing spiritual disciplines, then I would be more satisfied with myself, and I would be a better Christian."

"If I go to that new church, then I will feel like I used to feel when I first became a Christian."

"If I commit to serving more often or going on a mission trip, then God will answer my prayers."

Each "if" reveals lies at the bottoms of our hearts, lies so deep that we almost never put them into words. They function as an undertow whose presence silently shapes the surface of the water. Kyle and I have discovered that these lies are the problem, and they need to be uncovered and explored. To find healing, one must embrace what needs healing. Often it is our approach to God that needs healing most.

This book addresses these deeply abiding lies by helping to uncover how we hide them and why they thrive below the surface of our hearts. In much the same way I help those who come on retreat to open their hearts to the Lord regarding their broken expectations, so we encourage you to honestly assess how you view your relationship with God. Perhaps you picked up this book to answer questions similar to those of my retreat attendees: "How do I fix this?" and "How do I get that feeling back I used to have with God?" Our prayer for you is that you may have the ability to hear that these are the wrong questions. We are not interested in quick solutions, techniques, and formulas for getting you back on track, nor are we hoping to guilt you into the idea that you aren't doing enough and you should just get your act together.

We want to help you learn how to be with God. It seems so

simple, so central, and yet in the flurry of concerns that occupy our spiritual consciousness, is so easily overlooked. What does it mean to live with God? Sitting with this question requires prayer. It requires listening to God, waiting upon him, opening our hearts to his guidance, and fixing our eyes on his beauty. The answers cannot be found in a four-step solution, a new way to read an obscure passage of the Bible, or even by a rigorous commitment to try harder. The call of the Christian life is to abide in relationship with God. As such, we propose that the ground of the Christian life is prayer.

"So, is this a book on prayer?" No, not if by "a book on prayer" you mean a book that tries to get you back to praying like you used to, promises to rescue you from boredom in prayer with a new secret technique, or simply offers a list of different prayer styles. This is not another "book on prayer." As with every tool in the hands of fallen people, we wield good instruments to make idols. So is the history of Christian people with prayer. We make prayer another item on the Christian to-do list. We allow prayer to serve our idolatrous endeavors for fix-its and experiences. We allow prayer to undermine a relationship with God by using it as a mechanism to grant us the kind of life we want.

The Christian life is being with God who is always with us. When we are with our Lord Jesus Christ by the presence of his Spirit, we are given access to the Father (Eph. 2:18). In God's presence we find healing and joy. In God's presence we come to grasp ourselves, our world, and our calling. In God's presence we come *to know* the love of Christ that *surpasses knowledge* (Eph. 3:19). This knowledge is where life is found because it is knowing God personally, intimately, and deeply.

In the pages ahead, we invite you to develop a deeper and richer vision of life with God. Rather than simply affirming our preconceived notions or appeasing our felt needs, we offer a vision of *life with God from the ground up*. In a sense, we mean this quite literally. Our starting point will be the place where human life began—the dust (Gen. 2:7). From there we will tackle challenging questions that define the contours of our lives with God:

Who is God?

Who are we?

What does it mean to relate to him?

What does it mean to *be with* him?

Our earthbound hearts often move from these questions to more practical concerns, but in God's kingdom, these questions are as practical as it gets. These questions speak to issues at the heart of the Christian life—questions that have often been neglected in our quest to get on with fixing and/or experiencing. Our invitation to you is to push beyond the simple, narrow, and superficial to something that can sustain you through your journey in this world. This may not be an overnight process, but it can be entered into right here and now in your day-to-day life (which, by the way, is right where the Christian life is meant to be lived). Will you set out with us to develop a life with God that is biblically grounded, richly relational, and immanently practical? This is an everyday walking with the Lord named Immanuel—*God with us*.

As you read, you may notice that two main emphases come to the surface. In the beginning of the book, we focus our attention on what it means to be humble creatures dependent on our Creator for life and breath, as well as what it means to be broken. These discoveries take us to Jesus. Jesus takes on our humanness and our brokenness, our dust and our dustiness. He shows us what it means to be a creature made in God's image, and he rescues us from the dusty reality that now marks our lives as a result of sin.

As the book progresses, we turn our attention specifically and practically toward being with God in Christ. Here we develop a new way of viewing and experiencing prayer as the very means of being with the God who is always with us. This is not about learning to fix your spiritual life, but learning to come to God in the truth of yourself. It is learning to be a child before your Father.

The only way to enter into the deep questions of life with God is to do so prayerfully. Therefore the only way to read this book well is to read it prayerfully. You might be frustrated with prayer right now. You might find prayer lonely, foreign, and painful. You might even subconsciously avoid God in prayer. Nonetheless, pray. Ask God to unveil your heart in prayer. Ask him to teach you about yourself so that you can receive his grace more fully. Ask him to enlighten your heart to his life, work, and power. We encourage you to read this book as we wrote it—within the prayer of the psalmist: "Search me, O God, and know my heart! Try me and know my thoughts! And see if there be any grievous way in me, and lead me in the way everlasting!" (Ps. 139:23–24).

ONE

CREATED TO BE WITH GOD //

I (JAMIN) WAS doing all the right things. I was reading my Bible regularly. I was enrolled in several Bible classes. I was living a life of service. In fact, I was leading a ministry caring for the homeless in the city. Yet something was amiss. I had lived this way for several years, and all the feedback I received was positive. This must be what it means to be a faithful follower of Christ. This is what the Christian life is all about. Yet something about it didn't feel right. In truth, I was flat out bored. I didn't feel inclined to rebel or fall away from the faith; I simply felt a dissonance in my walk with God. I couldn't quite put my finger on it. I was tired of the to-dos, but I wasn't sure why. My faith felt hollow and tedious. What was going on?

During that season of spiritual malaise, I was invited on a retreat where I was forced to spend extended time in prayer. Not prayer *for* others. Not prayer *with* others. Silent, solitary, unscripted, deprogrammed prayer. I felt like a kid forced to play

1

a sport he knew nothing about. I was fumbling in the dark, trying to remember the rules, all the while forgetting to play and have fun. It felt awkward, shallow, and forced. I felt lost. After about an hour of silence, alone in the mountains, God and me, I realized that the dissonance I felt was a surface marker of a deeper reality. I discovered within my heart a profound disconnect in my relationship with God. As I prayed, I realized I wasn't really sure who God was, and for that matter I wasn't sure who I was. I tried to lean in to all the theological truths I knew, but they offered no help in the deafening silence of lonely prayer. In that moment of naked honesty, God provided a turning point.

Before that point I had certainly prayed. I prayed for friends in need. I prayed God would take away my sin and guard me from future temptation. I prayed God would give me the desires of my heart. All these prayers were conducted, unfortunately, with little relational attachment, and functioned more as a phone transaction with a somewhat friendly but unknown customer service representative. What I realized on that retreat was that, in a very real sense, I had rarely truly prayed.

As Eugene Peterson stated, "We discover early on that we can pretend to pray, use the words of prayer, practice the forms of prayer, assume postures of prayer, acquire a reputation for prayer, and never pray. Our 'prayers,' so-called, are a camouflage to cover up a life of non-prayer."[1] I had been living a Christian life of "non-prayer," and now I knew it. Prayer had become another thing to do. It was another bullet point on the list of "shoulds" and "oughts" for good Christian behavior. At its best, it had been dressed up as a spiritual discipline: as one practice on the list of many that mature believers are supposed to engage in. As a result, prayer became a place to be good.

Prayer became a place to perform.

Prayer became a place to get things done.

If I was honest, even those "non-prayer prayers" were few and far between compared to reading my Bible or engaging in other Christian activities. That was for one simple reason: prayer did not offer an obvious return on investment. I didn't feel smarter as a result of prayer. I didn't feel better about myself as I prayed. I didn't feel like I was getting much done. So I turned to things like service and church attendance to gain a sense of accomplishment.

All this betrayed a deeper and more insidious reality in my life. My desire for a felt experience of self-fulfillment was the driving force of my spiritual activity. The Christian life had become more about looking and feeling like a Christian than abiding in relationship with God. I was operating in the realm of seeming, not being. However, if the Christian life is most fundamentally about being with God, then prayer cannot be merely another activity on the list of good Christian behavior. Prayer must be a way of life. But this is not what I had signed up for. I thought I believed Christianity was about having a relationship with God, but in that moment, alone before Him, I came to realize that deep down I didn't truly desire God's presence.

Claiming that Christianity is about a relationship with God taps in to the provocative truth that God gives himself. The solution to the pain, suffering, evil, and vice that plagues our world is nothing other than the presence of the Creator. God's presence brings healing. This is such a big idea, and its implications are so far reaching, that we often accept something less instead. Rather than embracing the wildly provocative truth that God has given himself to us, we come to believe he functions primarily to give us other gifts.

That was my issue. I had clearly focused more on the other gifts than the gift of God himself. Rather than his presence, I wanted a felt experience, a sense of personal growth. I made the mistake of sin, which always seeks to turn God's presence into a mechanism or resource to make my life better. Rather than worshipping God, I worshipped myself. I wanted life on my terms, so I did what I thought God would want, thus cleverly obliging him to make life work for me.

Perhaps nothing is as subtle and deceptive as the ease with which our forms of worshipping God (reading the Bible, singing, partaking in the Lord's Supper, serving the poor, etc.) can be used for our own self-worship. This is so subtle and deceptive that we don't even know it is there. We can become aware of this self-worship when we pay attention to our desires. Our desires hint at subconscious beliefs we hold about life, God, and ourselves. These beliefs often surface when we enter God's presence. In His presence we come to realize how often we relate to him as a tool or resource in our quest for happiness, fulfillment, and meaning, rather than as the Lord who calls us to worship.

To be with the God who is always with you, you must pay attention to how you respond to unwelcome feelings concerning your life with God. For instance, when you see sin in your heart, do you beat yourself up before God in penance, as if your self-inflicted wounds will ensure God looks upon you favorably? Maybe you find yourself bored in church, disinterested with Scripture, or joyless in your giving, and you respond by acting as if you are content and happy. If we can't have the real thing, maybe pretending will work?

This is the fork in the road of our lives with God. To the left is a choice to use God to achieve the kind of life you want. It feels faithful because of how much cultural Christianity is sprinkled in, how much we can accomplish, and how important we are perceived to be in our church. To the right is a choice to receive the truth of yourself. This fork leads to the foot of the cross, where the only proper response is to bow a knee to God.

Whichever direction we take at the fork in the road is identified with a posture before God. The path on the left is a posture of control. There, we are the center, and our life dreams are sovereign. To the right, God is central, and we find ourselves called into his presence to know the freedom of being beloved. We take a knee before our Lord and trust that he receives us in the whole messy truth of ourselves because we rest on his self-giving.

Our posture in relationship to God unveils the deep realities of who we are and how we see God. We all know that physical posture communicates a lot about the nature of a relationship. Our body language toward others can send clear messages of affection or rejection, resistance or openness. When a friend turns to his phone to text message someone else while you are sharing your heart with him, it communicates something. When your child scuffs her knee, but physically refuses your attempts to comfort and care for her, it communicates something. These are broken postures. They are postures of rejection and pride rather than love and humility. In the same way, our hearts always take a certain posture toward God. We know what an open, honest, and willing posture before someone looks like. We can sense this in conversations with friends, children, or a spouse. We also know what it looks like to have someone shut down. We know when someone is handling us rather than relating to us, dealing with us rather than seeking to know us. When we seek ways to "get life right" on our own, that is identical with a posture of rejection. We are telling God that we do not need him, or even want him, but just want a better life.

Sin in our lives causes us to shy away from God's presence. Just as light chases away the dark, so God's light reveals more of ourselves than we are comfortable with—the light of God can leave us scrambling for the shadows. Often, our solution is to try to make God revolve around us, rather than finding ourselves in the gravitational field of his life. We pridefully invite God into our stories rather than humbly receiving the invitation to share in his.

God is relentlessly personal. In giving himself, God requires that we give ourselves. In giving himself, God opens the door for us to come clean about who we are. God wants more than pretending. Therefore, we are called to vulnerability before him, to be open to him in everything. Openness is always relational. It is an awareness that everything in life is done in the presence of God. We live in the presence of a God who took on our nature in Jesus Christ and broke open his own life for us in the sending of his Spirit.

It Was Very Good

At the outset of the biblical drama, we are confronted with a beginning where no beginning had been before. God, the eternal one, created all things from nothing. He did not create out of compulsion or coercion, but freely out of his abounding and gratuitous love. He spoke, and it was. He gazed upon creation, and it was *good*. Creation was good because he, the good One, was creating it. He created everything: light and dark, land and sea, plants and animals, and finally, man and woman.

Something different happened there at the end of the creation story. The rhythm of the poem was jolted just a bit. Man and woman were created in the very image of God himself and were given special authority over all he had created. From the beginning, man and woman were given a unique identity. We read in Genesis 1:26 that humanity was not simply *declared* like the rest of creation, but also *discussed* by the triune God: "Then God said, 'Let us make man in our image, after our likeness.'" [2] The conclusion of the act of creation sounded slightly different as well: "And God saw everything that he had made, and behold, it was *very* good" (Gen. 1:31, emphasis added).

Scripture already confronts us with a question of human identity, and we are not even beyond the first chapter. Who are Adam and Eve? Creatures, created in the image of God, created "very good." These identity markers probably generate more questions than answers. What does it mean to be a creature? What is it to be an image-bearer? What does it mean to be "very good"?

In Genesis 1, we sit in the theater watching the drama

unfold, but in Genesis 2 we are taken backstage. We are inside the action, and as a result we get a slightly different angle of the story. In parallel with the first scene, Genesis 2 offers new details about the creation of these image-bearers. We read, "then the LORD God formed the man of dust from the ground and breathed into his nostrils the breath of life, and the man became a living creature" (Gen. 2:7). Narrated with untamable tension, the text reveals two key concepts that shape human identity. First, "the LORD God formed the man of dust from the ground." We are dust—earthy and humble, finite and temporal. Second, he "breathed into his nostrils the breath of life, and the man became a living creature." We live on borrowed breath. We are *alive* in the most profound sense of the word—filled with the very breath that spoke creation into being. Within this tension is a status that is regal but lowly, significant but insignificant, unique but ordinary.[3] God looks upon humanity's frame of dust and says, "I formed you, I love you, and I delight in you." We are *beloved dust*.

Before we get ahead of ourselves, let's pause for a minute; there is something else in the story we should note. God culminated his activity on the sixth day of creation, and humanity was the final piece of the project. However, if we are not careful we will miss the crown jewel of the creation story as a whole. The culmination of creation was not the sixth day, but the seventh. "So God blessed the seventh day and made it holy, because on it God rested from all his work that he had done in creation" (Gen. 2:3). God's sabbath rest was truly the capstone of the project. It was this day of rest that God sanctified. This might strike us as a little odd. Why did God rest? Was he tired? Was he worn out? Did he need a break? No, God did not burn up all his energy. He didn't need a vacation.

We struggle with this because our culture equates rest with escape. Escape is about detachment, while true rest—as defined by God—is about attachment. It is about being with, moving in. God didn't check out. He did not desert what he had spoken into existence. By resting he ceased creating, but more importantly, his rest was an act itself. God's sabbatical rest was his decision to make the universe his resting place. His creation was his chosen abode. He would be present in the temple he had built. As John Walton stated, "God not only sets up the cosmos so that people will have a place; he also sets up the cosmos to serve as his temple."[4] God's rest was the King sitting down upon his throne: "This is my resting place forever; here I will dwell, for I have desired it" (Ps. 132:14).

The God who created everything lives with his creation. He has made his presence known. God's rest was God's decision to *be with* us. God is proclaiming: "I am here." God moved into his temple. That means God is not floating somewhere along the edge of the atmosphere, faintly present to his beloved dust. In Genesis, God established the garden of Eden as the seat of his rest. In the temple of God's creation, the garden of Eden was the holy of holies.[5] It was there that God walked and invited Adam and Eve to walk with him. Eden was not merely a garden for Adam and Eve, but was first and foremost *God's* garden (Isa. 51:3, Ezek. 28:13). In Eden, the heart of God's temple, he rested, fully present to his beloved dust.

The very moment we were raised from dust, we were invited to be with God. We were created for relationship with him. We were created for fellowship with the Creator of the universe. We were made within the cosmic temple that God chose as his resting place. He invited us to join him in his eternal rest, in his sacred home. God declared a profoundly loving yes to relationship with us.

What does it mean for us to be image-bearers in his temple? Traditionally, the last thing put into a temple is the image of the god for whom the temple was built. That image serves to represent the god to the world.[6] Likewise, with God's temple, he places humanity within it to image him to the world. To be the image of a relational God of love is to be called into God's life of love. It is no wonder Jesus claimed that the world will know his disciples based on our love (John 13:35). God made us to commune with him, to proclaim his presence based on who we are, which means we were created to relate with God in love.

It does not take long to encounter a crisis in the drama. Humanity rejects God's invitation into relationship. We say no to God's yes. Genesis 3 unfolds humanity's rejection of God and his presence. We all know the story. Adam and Eve rejected God's command not to eat fruit from the tree, because rather than depending on God, they wanted to *be* god. But something went wrong long before Adam and Eve actually ate the fruit. Something went wrong the moment Eve began to speak with the serpent. The nature of the conversation with the serpent was a profound sign that all was not well. Eve did not invite God into the conversation. The serpent had her on the ropes from the very beginning. She willingly accepted god-talk over God-relationship. As Eve dialogued with the serpent, we notice that the fellowship, communion, and rest in God, for which humans were created, were not on display. As Dietrich Bonhoeffer powerfully reminded us, this is "the first conversation *about* God."[7] Humanity exchanged being with God for talking about him, as if he was not actually present. We were not created to talk about God, but to be with him. From the moment of our creation, we were intended to live and move and have our being in him (Acts 17:28).

The good news is that, in the face of our no, God continues to say yes in Jesus. In Eden, we see God walking with his beloved dust. God's presence was tangible, allowing his creatures to see and touch the God who spoke into being all that we see and touch. Just as God entered the garden to be with his creatures, Jesus entered into the drama of redemption in the incarnation. Jesus invited us to life with God. Jesus was the image of the invisible God, a physical manifestation of God (Col. 1:15). Even more provocatively, in the incarnation Jesus became beloved dust. In becoming human, Jesus took on a new role. It is as if the writer, director, and producer of this divine drama took over the story from within, rewriting all that came before through the lens of redemption. By entering the drama in our place, and through his life, death, and resurrection, Jesus welcomed us back to our resting place with God. He invited us to participate as beloved dust once again. He called us into our roles in this great, living drama of redemption. To be caught up fully into this movement of God, we must learn to embrace a posture of openness to him in all that we do. We are not left alone by a vacant God, but called to live in the presence of the God who reveals himself to us.

An Apocalypse of Dust

Jesus used images of soil to talk about the nature of the heart—some hard, some full of thorns, some shallow, and others soft and able to receive the seed of God's Word (Mark 4:13–20). But the truth is that all our hearts are a mixture of these things. None of us are purely the soft in heart. When we come into contact with the greatness of God, we often subconsciously turn to things to protect ourselves from his presence. Maybe we focus our entire lives on service and ministry to avoid the vague and uncharted waters of prayer. Maybe we turn our Bible reading into a purely intellectual endeavor, not hearing God's Word proclaimed to us, calling us to himself—we're simply trying to be in the know. In some way, we all mimic Adam's and Eve's responses to the call of God—running behind bushes, looking for a place to hide.

In 1931 America's fertile plains were hit with what seemed at the time to be nothing short of the apocalypse. Clouds of dust, so thick you could not see five feet in front of you, covered the skies over what had been bountiful land decorated with golden wheat as far as the eye could see. Those that lived in Texas, Kansas, and Oklahoma called the clouds of dust "black blizzards." When a journalist visited and saw the drought-stricken and wind-depressed land, the phenomenon received its historical name, the "Dust Bowl." Many people died during the decade-long tragedy. Many more lost their livelihoods and were forced to escape to the West coast where, due to the Great Depression, conditions were no better than the land they had left. The clouds of dust reached all the way to the eastern seaboard, making their presence felt throughout the entire country. What caused the Dust Bowl? How could farmers go from record crops, promising abundant hope, to utter hopelessness at the reality of completely worthless land? The answer was a mixture of urgency, greed, technology, and technique.

The wide-eyed settlers had found land that was rich and buyers of their wheat that were willing to pay. Making money on their crops was a matter of speed and strategy. The faster they could plow the fields and plant the seeds, the quicker they could turn around and sell. This urgency caused them to turn toward new means to get the job done faster and with greater results. So they turned to the tractor, the newest technology on the farming market. They also turned to techniques that kept the soil free of the grass that had naturally grown in the land for years, which allowed them to plant immediately when the time came. However, when the drought arrived and was followed by wind, they realized their plans had backfired. It turned out that the natural, indigenous grass they destroyed by the deep plowing of the tractors was the only thing that could keep the soil in place when the harsh winds came. If only they had paid attention to the history of the land, the cycles of weather, and the unique dynamics of the soil, the Dust Bowl would have never happened. Technology and technique—the very things that brought immediate payoff—became their undoing. As John Steinbeck articulated in *The Grapes of Wrath*:

> Is a tractor bad? Is the power that turns the long furrows wrong? If this tractor were ours it would be good—not mine, but ours. If our tractor turned the long furrows of our land,

it would be good. Not my land, but ours. We could love that tractor then as we have loved this land when it was ours. But this tractor does two things—it turns the land and turns us off the land. There is little difference between this tractor and a tank. The people are driven, intimidated, hurt by both. We must think about this.[8]

You have been called to participate in the reality of God's work and to faithfully discern the soil of your heart. It is tempting to think we know what is needed. It is tempting to see the open plains of our hearts before us and think all we need is effort and strategy, technique and tools. However, the truth is, your heart is more complex than that. Our homespun theories on spirituality and growth are often nothing more than techniques that will untether our hearts from their foundation in Christ, being tossed to and fro by the winds of deceit. Instead, you must prayerfully ponder the conditions, get to know the soil, and learn how fruit is grown. This book focuses on the nature of our soil and the climate available to us in the light of God's grace.

What do we do when we grasp that our hearts are full of rocks, or that we have become untethered from Christ and are blown around like dust? What do we do when all our techniques have failed, even those promising a more exciting and fruitful Christian life? What do we do when we experience, more often than not, the hardness of our hearts rather than the softness? Life with God is from the ground up. It begins with a willing posture for God to till the soil of our hearts, embracing that only by grace, is the hard soil of our hearts penetrated. We must be open to the work of the Spirit within—illuminating the complexities of our hearts and calling us to be with God. We must embrace the truth that his Word is "living and active, sharper than any two-edged sword, piercing to the division of soul and of spirit, of joints and of marrow, and discerning the thoughts and intentions of the heart. And no creature is hidden from his sight, but all are naked and exposed to the eyes of him to whom we must give account" (Heb. 4:12–13). We need to trust the tools of God for his own tilling of our hearts, receiving the piercing blow of his Word as the hard soil receives a spade. If we put our trust elsewhere—in techniques and self-help—our tilling will throw dust in the air and in our eyes, blinding us to the truth of God and of ourselves.

This vulnerable posture is, paradoxically, where life is found. Life is not found in hiding from God, in showing God that you are good or convincing him or others that you are valuable. Life is found in real, honest, and vulnerable relationship with the God who calls you his beloved. As we embrace this posture of openness before God, the soil of our hearts will indeed be pierced by the living Word and searched by his Spirit. They will till the hard ground of your heart so that the living water can penetrate to the root system of your soul. Embracing a posture of exposure before God is diving deeply into the joy of communion with God, even when, like Adam and Eve, you feel naked and ashamed. This is a call to embrace God in times of abundance and in times of drought. It is a call to be always with the God who is ever present with you.

TWO

STUCK IN THE SANDS OF TIME //

> *On waking he found himself on the green knoll whence he*
> *had first seen the old man of the glen. He rubbed his eyes—*
> *it was a bright sunny morning. The birds were hopping*
> *and twittering among the bushes, and the eagle was*
> *wheeling aloft and breasting the pure mountain-breeze.*
> *"Surely," thought Rip, "I have not slept here all night."*[1]

THE STORY OF Rip Van Winkle has found a permanent place in the imagination of American culture. Washington Irving's short story tells the tale of a man named Rip Van Winkle who fell asleep before the Revolutionary War and magically awoke twenty years later, just after the war had ended. This unassuming man from a small village in the Catskill Mountains had traveled in time. While it has its place in our culture of legends and tales, *Rip Van Winkle* doesn't even touch the level of sophistication and extraordinary fantasy that our other tales of time travel—found in movies and books—have produced in recent history. Americans are clearly fascinated with this idea of being able to go back in time and explore the future. We love a good time-travel story. From H. G. Wells's time machine to Doc's DeLorean, we are captivated by what it would be like to overcome the constraints of time.[2]

This fascination with time travel has left the realm of pure fantasy and speculation and made its way into the laboratories of physicists who are exploring things such as time dilation and wormholes in an effort to uncover a means of traveling through time. However, as Stephen Hawking cautioned, until we meet "tourists from the future" we have no reason to believe in time travel.[3] Hawking's words do nothing to halt the unending fascination our culture has with the idea though. It seems as if every year there is a popular movie or a television show that explores the theme. It never grows old to us. Why is this? We love the idea of being able to transcend time. We want to be able to undo mistakes or pains of the past and to guarantee a particular reality for our futures. If we aren't hemmed in by the dictates of the clock, perhaps we can be more than simply human. So, the stories of time travel serve up exactly what we want—the potential to break the bounds of our creatureliness.

We must accept the truth of ourselves as creatures if we are going to embrace the Christian life as being with the God who is always with us. This may seem simple enough, but it is not. We are all deluded into believing that we are more than we are. These delusions of grandeur may be hidden in our subconscious, but there remains a powerful belief within our hearts that says, "If I have power and control, then life will go the way

I want it to." This is the subtle lie at the heart of our sin. It is the reason why self-help is such a temptation for us. It is exactly what we *want* to be true. We want to believe that we can fix our lives, and we want to believe that learning the right technique will save us. At the heart of idolatries such as these is the desire to have a different god from the God who has given himself to us in Christ Jesus. It is taking the deep and evil desires of our hearts, to make ourselves the center of existence, and generating an idea of a god we can serve—a god who will be impressed with us, a god who is on our side, and, maybe most importantly, a god we can control. As dust in the hands of our Creator, we have no such power or control.

While our brokenness can lead us to embrace the lies of self-help, there is another reason we lean this direction. Simply stated, we do not interpret reality well. More specifically, we do not interpret God's movements in our lives well.

A few years ago I (Kyle) was living in Scotland, and a pastor invited me to hear Eugene Peterson speak. I had never read anything Peterson had written, but I knew *of* him, so I thought I would go. He talked about ministry, about being with people and shepherding, and there was a lengthy question-and-answer time allotted. Pastor after pastor asked similar questions in different ways, but the heart of these questions was one foundational inquiry: "Things are not going well. Our churches are growing smaller and smaller. Please tell us what we can do about this."

I remember watching Eugene process several of these questions, and I recall the confused look on his face. After a while he simply said, "Look, we don't have a plan B. If we knew of a better way to present the gospel, then we would be doing it—that would be our plan A. But there is no other plan. We are called to be faithful to what the Lord has called us to. There is no plan B if you don't like the outcome."[4]

For many of us, the Christian life isn't going the way we expected. If we attend to the questions of our hearts, they can be summed up with: What is plan B? Plan A does not seem to be working, so there must be something wrong with it. It could be that there is something wrong with "plan A." Perhaps you have a misguided understanding of the abiding life, a view of the Christian life we are trying to correct with this book. But there is no plan B beyond this. If it isn't going the way you want it to, the right questions are not "What is wrong with me?" or "What is a better plan?" Rather, the right question is "What is the Lord doing here and now?" Our calling is not to make the life we want; our calling is to embrace the life God has for us. We often assume the latter must be the former, but it rarely is.

When you are unsatisfied with the Christian life, when you are overcome with dryness and boredom, the only question that really matters is: Lord, where are you in the midst of this? If you focus on the reason this is happening, you will become lost. Maybe it is because of your sin, but what can you do about that other than turn to your Lord? We misinterpret what the Lord is calling us to because many of us turn to self-help in the exact place the Lord is calling us to abide. In the midst of our sin we start thinking, *I'll do better next time, God.* Or, *I'll fix this soon, I promise.* Or even, *Let me prove to you I'm worth your sacrifice.* All these are nothing less than idolatry and self-help. They are idolatry because they are oriented to a god other than the

Christian God. They are self-help because they assume that God wants us to get our lives in order before he will be with us. These lies forget that it was while we were in our sin that he died for us, and that without him, we can do nothing (Rom. 5:8; John 15:5).

A lack of satisfaction in the Christian life is an opportunity to embrace that we are dust. Embracing the truth of yourself before God carves out space to be with God as his own beloved dust. Dryness in the Christian life is humbling because it reminds us of our constant need for God, and therefore it is grace. But it is not the only reminder of our need. All our limitedness, our frustrations with ourselves, and our inabilities are gifts from God. They are all moments of grace calling us to depend fully on God and to proclaim, "Without you I can do nothing!" Maybe this is an outburst of anger at your child, when you see an uglier side of yourself that you fear. Maybe it is the realization that you simply cannot, or will not, forgive someone for how he or she has wronged you, and that rejection of forgiveness makes receiving God's forgiveness impossible. Maybe it is simply the nagging suspicion that you have not accomplished enough in your life, and if you only grit your teeth a bit more you can make yourself valuable. All these things reveal the desire to be God, to assert your will against all your limitations. When we reject our limitedness, we are rejecting time itself—another of God's gifts of grace. One of the great lies of self-help is that we can assert our will over time and craft time to submit to our pleasures and desires. Rather than interpreting who we are correctly, we come to reject the call of time on our lives. While many of us seek out a plan B that will finally fix our problems, we fail to realize that those problems are invitations to repent of our idolatry and rest in the truth of who God is and who we are before him.

The Oppression of Time

Our desire to transcend time is a result of our brokenness. In our sin, we believe we can be like God, just as Adam and Eve bought into the lie that they, too, could be like God. In response to their sin, God said, "For you are dust, and to dust you shall return" (Gen. 3:19). While undoubtedly hard to swallow, those words should have held little surprise for Adam and Eve. They may sound odd to us. Perhaps harsh. We want to know why this happened. Why did God respond this way? Yet, to answer the "why" question, we must recognize there is a deeper question undergirding what has happened. We need to understand the real identity of the characters involved, and this necessitates not merely "why," but "who?" Who is God and who are we? These are the questions that matter most. If we explore the story of creation with fresh eyes, we discover who we are in the story of how we were made: "Then the LORD God *formed the man of dust from the ground* and breathed into his nostrils the breath of life, and the man became a living creature" (Gen. 2:7, emphasis added). We are dust. And due to sin, not only are we dust, but to dust we shall return. Somehow our origin became our destiny.

At the heart of this creation story is one glaring truth: we are creatures. God is Creator, and we are a part of his creation.

// "And out of the *ground* the LORD God made to spring up
every tree that is pleasant to the sight and good for food"
(Gen. 2:9, emphasis added).

// "Now out of the *ground* the LORD God had formed
every beast of the field and every bird of the heavens
and brought them to the man to see what he would call
them" (Gen. 2:19, emphasis added).

Humanity is of the ground just like the plants and animals. We
are deeply connected with creation. We have been created from
the same stuff. God drew a line in the sand (or perhaps in the
dust) and made it clear that there is a great chasm between God
and us.

We are not eternal beings, unbound by time.

We are not infinite, unbound by space.

We are not creators of our identity or reality.

We do not choose our time or our place.

Unlike God, we have a history. Our history can be traced
back like a family tree; it can be traced all the way down to
the dirt.

God, lest Adam forget his humble origins, highlighted
Adam's identity the very moment he named him. The Hebrew
word *Adam* derives from *Adamah*, which means "ground."
Adam most literally means "from the ground" or "earthling."[5]
When you meet these characters in the divine drama, there is
no mistaking who they are. They are named according to their
statuses. Quite simply, we humans are dust. We come from
dirt. But what does this mean? How do we respond? Perhaps
the words of John Calvin provide us with an initially helpful

answer: "He must be excessively stupid who does not hence learn humility."[6] Knowing you are dust should cause you to stand before your Maker in awe—in awe of God and in awe of his graciousness. Similarly, we might add, it is excessively foolish to embrace prayerlessness instead of a life of prayer. To know you are dust is to know you need to pray. To grasp one thing is to grasp the other.

Locked in History

My wife seems to remember everything. I mean *everything*: who sat next to her in kindergarten, or the color scheme of the first hotel room she stayed in as a four-year-old. I (Jamin), on the other hand, struggle to remember even recent events of my life. This contrast is most glaringly and painfully brought to light on days of importance in our relationship—mostly anniversaries. In spite of our differences in memory retention, we are both human. We are both limited in the scope of what we can access in our history because our history is just that, a *history*. It has a beginning. It is shaped by time. Even if my wife could remember every event of her life, she, like all of us, is unable to remember life before she was conceived. However obvious at first glance, this is a profound reality. It shapes who we are and who we are not.

I am a creature.

I am human.

I am temporal.

I am transient.

As James 4:14 tells us, "You are a mist that appears for a little time and then vanishes." I have not existed from eternity past. I am not the Alpha and Omega. I am not the one who is, who was, and is to come (Rev. 1:8). I am not God. I am not Creator. *I am dust.*

The creation account has made our status clear. God willed us into being; he has spoken us into existence. He didn't bump into us halfway through his creation of the universe and say, "Where did you come from?" Nor did he clone himself by breaking off a piece of his essence and call it humanity. We are not divine beings. We are other than God. We are creatures. We have a beginning. We have a history. Put differently, God is wholly other. He alone is Creator. He has no beginning. He is not bound by time. He has no history. As Karl Barth stated, "Prior to the emergence of the creature there is only the Creator, and prior to commencing time there is only God's eternity."[7] God makes this clear by revealing his name. "God said to Moses, 'I AM WHO I AM'" (Ex. 3:14). God's method in creation heralds this truth of our identity: "*Then the LORD God formed the man of dust from the ground* and breathed into his nostrils the breath of life, and the man became a living creature" (Gen. 2:7, emphasis added). From the very beginning God is telling us something about ourselves. Dust is a sign that we are created. It is an unalterable proclamation that we are less than he, for he has always been. And yet, shockingly, it is to this dust that God speaks, and to this dust that God listens.

The Fruit of Idolatry

In a world where every message attempts to remind us that we can rise above, that we won't die, and that the right product will help us turn the tides of time, we forget we are not in control. Our foolishness leads us to believe that we control life and have it on our terms. The great lie of life is that you can grasp power and control and create a life of meaning. The fruit of this foolishness is prayerlessness. Prayerlessness is forgetting who you are and what kind of drama you are in—that you are not on your own, isolated and alone, but live your life in him, through him, and with him. Prayerlessness is believing that you are more than dust and that time will bend to your will. Prayerlessness is always the fruit of idolatry. Prayerlessness is poor interpretation of reality, and it leads to a posture not fitting of who you are. This posture leads us to continually whitewash our lives while our hearts die within.

Time does not bind God, nor does it exclude him. God has always acted within human history. The clock does not condition his decisions. His will is not at the mercy of time. With the Lord, "one day is as a thousand years, and a thousand years as one day" (2 Pet. 3:8). He communicates himself within the bounds of our time and space, but he is not constrained by either. God's creation is receptive to his action without binding him in it. The Bible reveals the acts of God within human history, acts that bring creation alive with his presence. God is not only above and beyond, but "In him we live and move and have our being" (Acts 17:28). Just as we are created and not creators, we are bound by our creatureliness while God has unfettered freedom.

We need to be aware of how we respond to time in our day-to-day lives so we can access our hearts' deep belief about it. Do we shift our weight anxiously because the line for coffee is more than four people long? Do we judge certain people to be "a waste of our time," as if they were less than beloved of God? Our decisions concerning how we relate to time (or our denial of it) will come out in prayer. Until we accept the reality that we often reject our creatureliness, we will feel like we are doing something wrong in prayer. Prayer does not provide a feeling of productivity. Prayer refuses to be enveloped by our misguided views of time. Prayer refuses to be bound by our religion of time management. Prayer is not about work or efficiency. In prayer we certainly do something, but in a very real sense we do nothing. In short, prayer calls us to our creatureliness. It reminds us that we live in time. It calls us to rest in the profound truth that our productivity doesn't actually matter that much, because the Creator of the universe is sovereign over time.

In our brokenness we refuse to embrace our temporality. We try to finagle prayer into our grandiose vision of a productive life, a satisfying life, or a life without grief. In response, we gravitate toward techniques and practices in prayer. We find ourselves thinking, *There must be something I can do to guarantee prayer is a bit more exciting, productive, meaningful, or fulfilling.* Being with God is not considered valuable. We don't want to waste our time, and in order for our time to be "well spent," we have to have something to show for it.

And this is the rub. We believe, deep down, that being with God is a waste of time—that somehow attending to the God who created us, saved us, and provides for us is without purpose. It would be similar to viewing those "wasted hours" when you were dating your future spouse as purposeless. It was in those hours that you came to know each other, share life, dreams, passions, and probably failures, hurts, and fears. It was the long phone conversations that seemed to go nowhere and the humdrum dates that helped build the bond you now accept as love. Prayer is calling us to this kind of time, to "waste" our time with God in the same manner. As we "waste" time with God, we are opened to the profound truth that we are temporal creatures dependent on God. As time stands still in prayer, we realize just how much we have been trying to control time outside of prayer.

Every second of every day we should be aware of our condition as creatures stuck in time. Every minute, every hour, every month, and every year it is clear we are not eternal. For these realities (seconds, minutes, hours, days, months, and years) are boundaries. We are bound by time. Just as the sand of an hourglass pours forth enclosed in its glass walls, so do we, as dust, walk through life within the walls of time. In our fast-paced society, the tyranny of time is even more palpable as we rush from appointment to meeting to event. We feel our blood pressures rise as we sit in traffic, horrified by how much of our day is slipping through our fingers.[8] Every glance at a clock brings guilt for wasted time, anger for others wasting *our* time, and sometimes envy that others seem to have all the time in the world. Even outside of our manic and frenetic society, time is an unstoppable force in the world. It is a force that frames human existence. Time is given and taken away as it drifts past us with inevitable regularity. It is the facilitator of both opportunity and lost opportunity. It is a force that thrusts us into action and calls us to make choices. If, in our naivety, we doubt our enslavement to time, all we need to do is look at the clock and notice that the hands keep spinning. There is nothing we can do to slow time. There is nothing we can do to pause the seconds as they tick off into nonexistence. Our attempts to resist or reject time are as foolish as the sand of the hourglass trying to climb back up the slippery glass walls.

But this is the very thing that drives our lives. Stopping, slowing, or pausing time is the pastime of God's broken creatures. As animals continue on, embracing the circle of life that leads to their demise, humanity turns a deaf ear to reality to seek fantasy. We posture ourselves in rebellion against our creaturely identity by doing everything we can to control time. We use clothes, surgery, cars, jewelry, style, luxury, and nearly anything else to pause the inevitable flow of time. The invention of the clock itself is a sign of humanity's attempt to control time. As Neil Postman quipped, "The inexorable ticking of the clock may have had more to do with the weakening of God's supremacy than all the treatises produced by the philosophers of the Enlightenment . . ."[9] Clawing our fingers in the dirt from which we were made, we seek to slow time as it drags us on. Subtly following Eve's example, we believe that we, too, can be like God. We can be unbounded by time, unfettered from the reality of our creatureliness. We can control our fate.

The Space of Grace

You can only embrace your temporality by walking with God through your attempts to control your life and time. As we experience our brokenness—our lustful hearts, our envy at a friend's success, or our anger at other drivers on the road—we must use these realities as opportunities to take a posture of dependence on God. How do you respond to your sin? How do you respond to Scripture when it touches a particularly painful reality of your life? It is important not to get overwhelmed by our brokenness, nor should we ignore it. Instead we should use it to proclaim, "Without you I can do nothing!" and "I believe; help my unbelief!" (John 15:5 (paraphrased); Mark 9:24). Only in this embrace can we come to walk in the way of Christ. It is here where we come to embrace our own neediness. Only in grasping that we are dust can we grasp our total need for surrender. Only in the embrace that our lives are brief and fleeting do we grasp that our time, however limited, has been sanctified by God in Christ (James 4:14). Time is the space of grace, calling us to silence before him, humbly seeking after him, and waiting upon him and his timing.

This is, of course, in sharp contrast to the world. What is heralded as virtuous in our world is frequently outright rebellion. Often our sinful strategies to control reality are disguised as signs of maturity or responsibility, such as time-management workshops and daily planners. We religiously submit to our calendars, and we craft to-do lists as though they were sacred documents. We adopt strategies in hopes of overcoming the harsh boundaries of time. All the while we are going against the grain. We are resisting reality. We are rejecting truth. We are denying who we are. Rather, the call of God is to go with the grain. It is a call to live in the truth of who we are as dust. All creation must submit to the rhythms of created reality. We must sleep. We must eat. We must breathe. To live against this grain is foolishness.

Believing that controlling time will grant freedom actually enslaves us to it. This is the great lie. But if we embrace our boundaries, we can experience freedom as God intended. As we live the Christian life, we are called to posture ourselves as temporal creatures, accepting our created status as a gift.

Sleep is an excellent litmus test of our posture toward time. Often, we view sleep as superfluous—wasted space that can be used if we determine more time is needed to accomplish a certain task. Every night millions of people around the world stare blankly at their TVs to avoid the reality that sleep is next on the day's docket. Embracing our call to be creatures entails embracing sleep as a fundamental aspect of our vocation. We are called to rest and respect our bodies. In this sense, for many believers, sleep is a profound, spiritual practice reminding us on a daily basis of the truth of our identity as creatures. In sleep we are laying down our bodies as living sacrifices before the Lord (Rom. 12:1). This, too, can be an aspect of our worship of God.

I (Jamin) have come to notice in my own life a great temptation to rebel against my temporality. It is a temptation to go against the grain. It is an astoundingly subtle temptation. There is a deep belief that I can master time. I subconsciously believe that being bound by time is a hindrance to all that I "should" accomplish. This belief surfaces at various moments, but it's most vivid when I return home from a long day at work. My wife often asks me about my day, and all too often I reply, "I got nothing done today." Of course, this statement is ridiculous. But within my fantasy I am convinced that I should accomplish all the projects I believe are significant in one eight-hour day. As my wife prods for clarification, I respond, "There just isn't enough time in the day," or "If I had been a little more focused, I would not have lost so much time." There are only a few days when I feel satisfied with how much I accomplished. I have not fully received my temporal limitations. I have not embraced the truth that life's work is not done in one day, and quite often it isn't even accomplished in a lifetime.

As years seem to get shorter with every new year of life, and as we feel the effects of time on our bodies and health, we can either reject reality in foolishness or embrace God in freedom. Time itself may feel like wrath to you, as it does to me sometimes. Time may be the constant reminder of all that you want to forget. But time itself is God's gracious call to his beloved dust to rest upon him and know his peace. Only by being with God, who is always with you, can you embrace this truth. Only by being with God will you come to see that "losing your life"—laying down your attempts to control time—is the way to saving it.

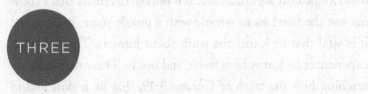

THREE

UNLIMITED LIMITATION //

MY SON DOES not want my help, but this was not always the case. I (Jamin) can vaguely remember when he *always* wanted my help: help figuring out how to get his spoonful of Cheerios to his mouth without spilling or help coaxing a desired toy out of a crevice. But now my help is not welcome. The mere mention that Dad might be of assistance is met with anxious resistance. I often find it difficult not to swoop in and solve dilemmas when his limitations loom large. I know myself well enough to know I am tempted to try to fix situations regardless of whether or not my help is desired. Conventional wisdom tells us that by allowing our children to struggle through small things, they learn to accomplish them on their own and develop self-confidence.

As it turns out, conventional wisdom is not the only reason I should allow my son space to figure things out on his own. There is an even deeper spiritual reality at work. As difficult as it is for me to allow my son the space he desires, he needs the opportunity to discover his *finitude*. Giving him space to tackle challenges on his own not only engenders healthy self-confidence, but it also develops healthy *self-awareness*. It is not out of cruelty that I allow my son the freedom to wrestle with a puzzle piece, but because it is vital that he learns the truth about himself. Through such experiences he learns he is feeble and needy. These moments are teaching him the truth of Genesis 3:19, that he is dust and to dust he shall return. He is learning that he is finite. He is slowly learning to posture himself as a creature of dust. This is the posture that we are all learning to embrace or reject.

I am a creature.

I am finite.

I am not all-powerful.

I am not all-knowing.

Unfortunately, as adults, we still have not learned that we are finite. Regardless of countless failures, mistakes, and frustrations brought on by our weakness, we still turn to independence, self-help, and self-empowerment as the answer to our problems. Only after we have exhausted all other options do we change our posture. Only then do we pray. So we must ask, do we embrace the truth that we are dust? Do we embody postures of dependence and neediness? More often than not, the answer is no. We may use language of neediness or even tack on a "Lord willing" to our plans for the future. But beneath the surface we still believe that life is practically in our hands. It is still up to us. In effect, we are often willing to admit we might need a little bit of help, but once God gets us started, we can take things from there. We reject dependence because, like Eve, the idea that we, too, can "be like God" is just too tempting an offer. At the core of all our hearts resides the lie that if only we had power and control, then we could have the life we've always wanted. So we reject dependence and opt for self-help, the great lie of the modern age.

Learning our finitude is only fully possible once we meditate on God's infinity. Staring into the depths of God's greatness, depths we can only look into with wonder and amazement, helps us locate ourselves within his creation. As Psalm 33:6–8 declares, "By the word of the LORD the heavens were made, and by the breath of his mouth all their host. He gathers the waters of the sea as a heap; he puts the deeps in storehouses. Let all the earth fear the LORD; let all the inhabitants of the world stand in awe of him!" God is Creator. God is infinite. He alone is all-powerful. He alone is all-knowing. He alone is God.

We might not have life figured out. We might not even have ourselves figured out, but if we come to grasp that we are finite, we have come a long way. Doing so leads us to the unimaginable fact that we are not necessary. We are not needed. There was a time when we did not exist—a time when we were not. This should not lead us to wallow in our insignificance, but should lead us to find awe in the creative grace of God. Doing so locates us correctly within the broad scope of the divine drama we find ourselves in. Our fragility should lead us to trust in the One who is infinite. Our brokenness and weakness should lead us to glory in the fact that God listens to his dust and calls us beloved. Our weakness should lead us to proclaim God's praise. It should harness reverence and delight in our hearts rather than frustration and discouragement. Above all, as we come to know God, we must come to accept a posture of humility, dependence, and love so that we, too, can receive Jesus' message to Paul, "My grace is sufficient for you, for my power is made perfect in weakness" (2 Cor. 12:9).

Fantasy Life

Since the plague of sin descended upon humankind, desperation to find meaning has ushered in idolatries of every kind. We try to avoid hearing that we are dust. We try to avoid hearing about our finitude, our temporality, and the boundaries that surround us. Instead, we create lives of fantasy, pretending we can generate our own identities and realities. Instead of receiving and embracing our calling as creatures, we seek to transcend what we are on our own. In Genesis 11 we encounter a story declaring the finitude of man and the glory of God. It is a story that teaches us that we cannot ascend to God, but rather God descends to us. This story highlights our idolatrous desire to find freedom *from* our creaturely reality and points us to find it *within* the goodness of God's creation. This story reveals the line drawn in the dust between Creator and creatures. It is the story of the Tower of Babel.

The people of Babel had a grandiose vision. They sought to have life on their own terms. They had great faith in their capacity to break free of the bonds of a dust-shaped life. Fundamentally rejecting their finitude, they believed they could ascend to heaven by building a tower. At the heart of their idolatry was the desire to make their name great rather than God's name: "Then they said, 'Come, let us build ourselves a city and a tower with its top in the heavens, and let us make a name for ourselves, lest we be dispersed over the face of the whole earth'" (Gen. 11:4). The descendants of Adam and Eve were rejecting their finitude in every way possible, choosing to embrace a posture of power over weakness.

The builders' refusal to embrace their identity as finite creatures did not go unnoticed by the infinite Creator. Their actions reached heaven, but this was only because heaven came down. Just when we think that their quest to rise from the dust by their own power would work, God showed up. In fact, quite significantly, God came *down*. The entire passage centers around one verse that declares the truth of humankind's identity and God's identity: "And the LORD came down to see the city and the tower, which the children of man had built" (v. 5). God confused them and scattered them. The quest to eradicate their finite identity was radically unsuccessful. The people of Babel learned the hard way that the distance between Creator and creature was great. The only words that could fit such a realization came from Abraham just a few chapters later in the book of Genesis: "Behold, I have undertaken to speak to the Lord, I who am but dust and ashes" (Gen. 18:27). God reminded them that they were created and he was Creator. He reminded them that they were finite and he was infinite.

We, of course, are not any different than the people of Babel. Our culture does us no favors in the quest to embrace our finitude. Our Western credos are oriented toward the complete rejection and avoidance of our finitude. "If you set your mind on something, you can accomplish it." "If you work hard, you can overcome." Even the American dream has been used to prop up our self-glorifying and dust-rejecting endeavors.

What more is the "pursuit of happiness" than the quest to create the life we want and to reject any "evil voices" of dissent that tell us hard work doesn't guarantee us such a life? Think about the narratives of success in our country. We tell stories of people overcoming all obstacles by willpower and determination to succeed. These stories validate our most primal sin, pride. Disguised as hope and encouragement, these narratives perpetuate the lie that we are all we need. We live against the backdrop of these stories and come to affirm this radically subhuman truth that if I only work hard enough, I can have life on my terms, and, in fact, I *deserve* to have life on my terms. We "pull ourselves up by our bootstraps" to transcend what holds us down. All the while, God gazes upon our efforts to construct a life that rejects dependence and humility in favor of independence and pride.

Just like the Tower of Babel, prayer often becomes a place to try and force God's hand. Rather than accepting our powerlessness over God—that nothing we can do will push him, move him, or force him to make life the way we want—we subconsciously come to believe saying the right thing or doing the right thing will make it happen. We have an agenda, so we look for ways to get it done. When my (Kyle's) daughter wants to avoid something inevitable, such as going to sleep, she often turns to us through tear-soaked eyes and just says, "Pray?" She knows that Mom and Dad don't turn down prayer requests. But there is no deceiving us. We pray, but we know that this is a way for her to get her way. This is something she has learned to do to try to make life the way she wants. It is often no different for us.

While our techniques are probably more subtle than my

daughter's, they are not more advanced. The rejection of our finitude is nowhere more obvious than in our worship and dependence on modern technology.[1] Our newfound technology offers the promise and hope of transcending our limitations. With godlike strength and ease we are able to create, retrieve, and share. In short, technology is our mechanism of control. It provides us hope. We believe, if only we utilize our technological savvy to its fullest capacity, integrate it efficiently, and continue to push it toward its greatest potential, it will enable us to transcend the brokenness of our world. Each new device and product holds promises of god-like transcendence: talk to anyone, anywhere, anytime; find information in minutes that otherwise would require days of research. Imagine the moments when our computers crash or we lose our smartphones. A great wave of finitude comes rushing in. Our flight into the infinite comes crashing to the ground. How will we accomplish what we need to do? What if we are missing out on something? Without our technology we are merely human, and that is a scary prospect indeed.

Technology, of course, is simply a medium. That said, modern technology has an interesting way of revealing our idolatry. Whether it is the rise of online friendships matching the decline of real friendships, or the rise of savvy techniques and the decline of spiritual discipline and discernment, we are a people much more interested in things that will keep us excited about our lives than entering into the fray and messiness real life entails. It is not exciting in prayer when we are overcome by our finitude, our brokenness, and the deafening silence. We don't want to be confronted with the shadows of our hearts, so we often use prayer as an attempt to hide from them. But it is in these shadows that God calls us to be with him. Our dependence on techniques and technologies reveals how little being with God is the focus. We treat God like a genie in a bottle—someone who we can use for our own advantages, rather than have a relationship with. God calls us to himself, when what we really want is magic.

Surprised by Frailty

Prayer is fundamentally relational, and therefore it is humanizing. In prayer we are awakened to the calling of our humanity. Seeking to be independent, in control, and powerful dehumanizes us and leads to the dehumanization of others. These are the places where one's soul goes to die. These efforts lead only to a desert of isolation. Prayer, in contrast, is a place of abiding. In prayer we are called to be with the sovereign Creator of the universe as finite creatures. We are called to posture ourselves as those in need of the all-powerful and all-knowing One. We do not simply embrace this posture by sheer willpower or consistent reminders. To be with God in the truth of our finitude can only be learned in prayer. It is, in many ways, synonymous with prayer. When we encounter God in truth and have the reality of our creaturely limitations mirrored back to us, then we come to experience our finitude in grace.

Our lives are filled with experiences that mirror the reality that we are finite. Some are fleetingly presented to us throughout the mundane corridors of our lives, and others are earth-shattering events that alter our existence. Perhaps we cannot remember an important meeting we scheduled. Perhaps we discover we are powerless to keep our teenage child from making bad decision after bad decision. We all have strategies to avoid seeing the truth that we are finite. We know the easiest ways to distract ourselves and escape reality. We know people we can go to who are sure to tell us what we want to hear, and we have tried-and-true psychological techniques that will help us prop up whatever false selves we need to embrace in order to avoid the reality that we are dust. We know deep down that these strategies will fail in true prayer, so when we go to God, we simply rattle off a list of things we want, pepper it with requests for others to relieve our feelings of guilt, and get out as fast as we can to avoid the experience of failure and brokenness before God.

Our great mistake is to see our brokenness, our finitude, and our sin as things that keep us from God rather than as opportunities to throw ourselves at the foot of the cross and grasp his grace. These opportunities should be embraced, not because our sin is not important, but because God has proclaimed "It is finished" from the cross. When we lust *yet again*, when we gossip *yet again*, when we erupt in anger at our kids *yet again*, we are confronted with our inability to eradicate such darkness from our lives. Healing comes only by walking with God through our brokenness, never by avoiding it and pretending it isn't there. Unfortunately, instead of resting in God in these times, we turn to self-help, buying in to the lie that God wants us to fix our lives before we depend on him. We often use these strategies of avoidance when we are faced with the reality that we are unable to produce any genuine spiritual transformation on our own. In moments of honesty we come to grasp that no amount of self-discipline or theological acumen erases our sinful habits. We are faced with the truth that we are helpless to *truly* enact change. In fact, we are limited in our ability even to understand what needs to be changed, much less change it. All this should lead us to prayer, to the God who knows we are dust yet calls us to himself.

A few years ago I (Jamin) was faced with my finitude vividly and painfully: I lost my job. I didn't see it coming. I had just become a first-time homebuyer. To add further complexity, I was caring for my then four-month-pregnant wife who was on strict bed rest with our first child. I felt exposed, ashamed, and angry. As I listened to my boss explain the reasons for my release, a bit of the finitude crept to the surface. I couldn't magically fix the anemic church budget. I had no power to change the decision that would inevitably reverberate in every area of my life. The realities mirrored my limitations. I didn't see it coming, and I couldn't stop it. Yet I still held on to some *natural* hope. I was able to extinguish the initial realization of my finitude by envisioning other job possibilities and strategizing how I would get an even better job. My own pride did not allow the truth that I was dust to be truly recognized and experienced.

Before long, losing my job unraveled into a season of unemployment. Job opportunity after job opportunity would come and go. Each potential job would lead to multiple rounds of interviews, inevitably hearing that I was a "great candidate," but someone else was a "better fit." As each potential opportunity evaporated, my wife's due date crept closer and closer. I was going to have to provide for a wife and a child. Somehow, amid all the other concerns, the reality of being responsible for a family had not captured my attention completely. The truth of my finitude bubbled to the surface again, and this time it poured over the edge. At first I tried to avoid the tidal wave. I focused on all the avenues I had not yet explored and began to craft a new plan. But I could not fix my situation with self-engineered hope and reinvigorated willpower. Consequently, I moved to hopelessness and despair. I would dwell on what happened and then beat myself up for not finding another job. I would escape and avoid facing the truth by reading a book or perusing the Internet. Eventually, I was a tornado of frailty, insecurity, and shame. I was seeing the truth, but still not receiving it. I had run the gamut of strategies to avoid actually embracing the reality of my finitude. Then the strategies of managing and avoiding my situation were stripped away. Within that place of chaos, I began to hear the call of God and the truth he had for me. He was teaching me the truth of my identity—that I was limited, needy, and feeble. Ultimately, I could not control my world. All my best efforts could not guarantee me anything. I was not master of *my* universe, let alone *the* universe. He was teaching me that I am a creature and he is the Creator. He was teaching me that I am dust.

My prayer life during that time went from one end of the spectrum to the other. When I first lost my job, I was praying very little. Why pray? I needed to work my contacts and sharpen my résumé. However, as I struggled to find a job, I began to enter in to prayer. Even still, I was not entering in to prayer as one who was finite and in need of God, but rather as one who was more than capable of managing his life. Prayer was simply another one of my resources—it couldn't hurt to have a little help from God. I was still in control. It was still ultimately up to me. It wasn't until I was in a position of desperation that I began to truly pray. I began to cry out to God. I voiced my hurt. I shared my fears. I listened for God's guidance. Ultimately, I came to God as a finite creature, one who was desperate and needy. It was in prayer that I came not only to embrace my finitude, but to celebrate it, and rest in the truth that the Creator of the universe was with me. I came to celebrate the truth that I wasn't God, but indeed I was known by God. In many ways, it was a violent lesson for me. I wrestled with God to maintain the delusion that I was in control of my life. By his grace God wounded me so that I might learn that limping with him in my finitude was better than running on my own.

My failure to embrace God immediately, and instead turning to my own ability, is something we all experience. We cease to grasp how finite we are. When we are confronted with the loss of a job, a broken relationship, financial problems, death, sickness, frustration, and hurt of any kind and we create strategies to deal with life and try to generate a better existence, we end up dehumanizing ourselves and others. When we reject what we are, we become less than what we were made to be. When we reject dependence on God, we usually do so because we believe that independence is the height of human achievement. Eventually, we will be reminded that we are dust. It may be when our bodies decay from old age, or it may happen much sooner, but the truth of God's world is that the true human life is a life of prayer.

In prayer we learn what it is to be human. Prayer is the heart of a genuinely *human* existence. In prayer we learn to live in dependence on God; we learn to find life outside of ourselves in another person, Christ. In prayer we struggle to embrace our finitude, and therefore prayer is frustrating. We fail to see that we are using prayer as a means to something else, and therefore fail to see that prayer is frustrating because we are using it and rejecting relationship. We are like my little girl who wants to use prayer to get life on her terms. True prayer, instead, leaves us undone before a holy, powerful, and all-knowing God. Coming before God in truth will always unveil our finitude, or else we fail to grasp who God is and who we are. Standing before God entails grasping that all life should be lived in dependence on him. We do not simply realize this truth, but come to embrace it in our hearts. As we receive God's wisdom in prayer, we learn that life is intended to be lived in dependence on him.

Just as the world seeks to seduce us to try and manipulate time, it also claims we can rise above our finitude. We can be immortal. When you hear the greatest professional athletes of our day talking about their legacies, they often equate championships with immortality. It will always be remembered, they think, therefore their memories will live on even when they are gone. This, of course, is foolishness. Trying to defeat our limitedness is fighting against our nature and seeking to live against the grain of who we are. It is the lie that has echoed throughout human history—we can be like God. Human history is, in many ways, the story of humanity seeking to be like God on its own, with an important plot of hope where God himself descends into time to provide a way to be like him. But we do not see the abundant life he offers; we see death and foolishness (John 10:10). Jesus claims we must lose our lives in order to save them (Matt. 10:39) and be last in order to be first (Mark 10:44). But even if our hearts cry out, "This is a hard saying; who can listen to it?" (John 6:60) we need to proclaim with Peter, "Lord . . . You have the words of eternal life, and we have believed, and have come to know, that you are the Holy One of God" (John 6:68–69). True life is embracing Jesus, which means that true life is embracing the grace he has given us in our finite, limited existence. In all this we must learn to accept the posture of waiting upon the Lord.

FOUR

HIDING IN THE DUST //

I (KYLE) HAD a pet chinchilla when I was a kid. His name was Dusty. Chinchillas, if you aren't familiar with them, are little bunny-like rodents with a nice temperament and an incredibly soft fur coat. What most people don't know about chinchillas is that their natural habitat is very dry, and they don't bathe in water, but in dust. We kept a large bin of chinchilla dust in my room (Yes, there is such a thing!), where Dusty would take his daily bath when I let him out of his cage. The dust was thick and soft, and he would hop in and stand for a moment like a child gazing around a toy store. Then, for the next five solid minutes, he would roll and spin around in the dust. The dust would go flying. Afterward, just as at the beginning, he would stop and zone out for a minute with a satisfied look on his face, as though dust was the remedy for all life's struggles.

Like most boys in elementary school, I tended not to notice the messes I made. Add to that the dust-catapult in my room, spinning dust to the farthest reaches of my space, and what you get is a boy with no regard for dust. A fine veil of dust covered every item in my room as though it had been locked up for decades. Even to this day I tend not to notice dust. In the same way, our lives are pervasively dusty. It tends to coat every surface and crevice of our souls, often unnoticed.

It is important that we make a clear distinction of terms at this point. Dust, which we have discussed in the first three chapters of this book, refers to our status as creatures. We are finite and temporal. God raised us from the dust of the earth. It is central to who we are. It is humbling, but not *bad*. It is part of our being that God deemed "good." In this chapter we will take a turn and talk about a new concept: dustiness. What does it mean to be dusty?

The way of dustiness is the way of sin and death.

The way of dustiness is marked by prideful autonomy.

The way of dustiness is a rejection of what it means to be fully human.

The way of dustiness is a move away from relationship with God.

The difference between being dust, according to God's creative design, and being dusty is an important one. God formed us from dust in his image and called it very good, but we rejected this image for what is base and beneath us. We were given life as God's beloved dust, and we rejected it for the way of death. God called us as dust, but he never called us to be dusty. We are indeed called to humbly embrace our earthly origin, but also our heavenly calling, the way "from above" (James 3:15). Dustiness is our instinctive grasp of the lower in rejection of the higher. When we embrace the way of dustiness, we say no to depending on God as creatures, and we seek to rise above our creaturely status by our own power. This is the way of prideful autonomy we witnessed previously in the story of the Tower of Babel. Dustiness is to live as if God answers to you, rather than you to God.

The tension between dust and dustiness constantly plays out in the Christian life as the temptation to rely on ourselves. In so doing, we fail to rest solely upon God. Embracing that we are dust means that we cannot generate an identity of self-importance. It's hard to brag about dust. Dustiness is, in contrast, the temptation to generate an identity from within, proving to the world, God, and even ourselves that we are valuable. The way of dust embraces the truth that our value is found in God's love and grace. As such, the Christian life never leaves the cross. The cross is not simply where we become saved, but is now our place of rest. We do not come to the Lord needy and then become self-sufficient as we mature in the faith. We should always maintain a posture of neediness before the Lord, because he is the fountain of life, and we are the thirsty ones. The subtle lie of dustiness is that the Christian life is in our power to live, and therefore everything ends up revolving around us. In the modern world where self-centeredness is something of a trend, this is a dangerous lie indeed.

The Dusty Road

At the very beginning of the divine drama narrated in Scripture, we encounter two key characters who have been created from the earth, Adam and Eve. By creating them from the earth, God made it clear from the beginning that Adam and Eve were not gods, but creatures. The surprising twist in the story was that the people made of dust were also made in God's image. They were dust loved by the Creator and called to commune with him in eternal Edenic splendor. However, a chapter later we read, "For you are dust, and to dust you shall return" (Gen. 3:19). Like a deflated balloon careening back to earth, right when the dust began to grasp its beloved status, it plummeted back to its source. Something tells us this is not good news. What happened?

> Now the serpent was more crafty than any other beast of the field that the LORD God had made. He said to the woman, "Did God actually say, 'You shall not eat of any tree in the garden'?" And the woman said to the serpent, "We may eat of the fruit of the trees in the garden, but God said, 'You shall not eat of the fruit of the tree that is in the midst of the garden, neither shall you touch it, lest you die.'" But the serpent said to the woman, "You will not surely die. For God knows that when you eat of it your eyes will be opened, and you will be like God, knowing good and evil." So when the woman saw that the tree was good for food, and that it was a delight to the eyes, and that the tree was to be desired to make one wise, she took of its fruit and ate, and she also gave some to her husband who was with her, and he ate. (Gen. 3:1–6)

God had already warned them that the result of sin would be death (Gen. 2:17). They knew they had sinned. They did what God had commanded them not to do. They ate from the tree. Rather than embracing the way of beloved dust, they embraced the way of dustiness. Rather than clutching God above, they grasped for the earth below. Rather than finding life in God, they tried to find it within themselves and the creation they were meant to steward (Gen. 1:29).

The initial "dust bath" of Adam and Eve sprayed dust all over the garden and eventually the world. Dust would quickly settle on every object and crevice in the temple God had created, much as it did within my childhood bedroom. As the story continues, we see humankind tread down the path of dusty worldliness—self-reliance, rejection of relationship, pride, and ambition. There is a sense in the Genesis narrative that Adam and Eve and their descendants became more beastly—less human in its proper sense. The first sin was an inhumane act, not against others, but against themselves. Sin makes us less than what we are and grasps for what is beneath us. This initial act of self-dehumanization led immediately to the serial dehumanization of others, from Adam attempting to push the blame onto Eve, to Cain killing his brother. Humankind, endowed with the image of God and given the grace of fellowship with him, turned to acts that were not proper for creatures called beloved and destined for eternal life with God. Instead, they grasped onto realities below them. They embraced the way of dustiness.

Humanity's base desire to bathe in dust, to wallow in the filth, has turned the table on God's gifts, rejecting the dependence, communion, and fellowship he provides. Being dusty advances a human-centered view of reality, where independence, self-will, and domination become the central virtues (James 3:16). Dustiness is the dehumanization that runs rampant through our lives to everyone around us. Dustiness is a rejection of God's call to be with him as his people by once again believing the serpent's lie: you can be like God.

We all experience this dusty reality in our lives. We try to use people (treating them as less than human) to get our own way. It leaves us desperate in prayer, trying to use God to fix ourselves. Ultimately, just like Adam and Eve, we find that we do not want to be with God at all; we want to take life into our own hands and be like God. We don't want to believe that we are dust, finite, and temporal, so we generate ways to be the Creator, to control time and to have life on our terms. The life of dustiness is idolatry. The life of dustiness rejects God as he has revealed himself to us and attempts to turn him into another resource used to get what we want. Dustiness is our rejection of God, and it leads us to use anything in our power to hide from him.

Hide and Cover

This way of dustiness is not something that simply happened to us—it is a reality that continues to radically form our lives. As we see with Adam and Eve, it forms how we respond to God:

> Then the eyes of both were opened, and they knew that they were naked. And they sewed fig leaves together and made themselves loincloths. And they heard the sound of the LORD God walking in the garden in the cool of the day, and the man and his wife hid themselves from the presence of the LORD God among the trees of the garden. But the LORD God called to the man and said to him, "Where are

you?" And he said, "I heard the sound of you in the garden, and I was afraid, because I was naked, and I hid myself." He said, "Who told you that you were naked? Have you eaten of the tree of which I commanded you not to eat?" The man said, "The woman whom you gave to be with me, she gave me fruit of the tree, and I ate." Then the LORD God said to the woman, "What is this that you have done?" The woman said, "The serpent deceived me, and I ate." (Gen. 3:7–13)

Sin spreads like a plague. In a meager attempt to handle their folly, Adam and Eve wove together leaves to cover themselves. This act was a manifestation of their hearts. They felt exposed. Sin had opened up an unknown reality, and their subconscious reaction was to cover from each other and to hide from God.[1] What we see burgeoning forth from humankind are strategies to deal with their dusty situation. These strategies do not address the heart of their problems, but simply attempt to control the fallout. In the case of Adam and Eve, their strategy was to hide and cover. For all of us, dustiness will cause sin to burst out of our hearts demanding that we hide our faces from the living God. This will manifest itself throughout every aspect of our lives. It may entail projecting an exaggerated personality, building an identity solely on vocational success or social influence, or even using religious fervor and discipline to serve as a smoke screen for our true depravity. Once humanity's life with God was ruptured, our intuitive solution was to do whatever it took to feel secure and fulfilled. In the presence of a holy God, that means hiding.

We all, of course, know what it's like to feel exposed. We

know what it's like to have the light reveal the dark places we have been trying to hide. In those times questions of right and wrong rarely enter our minds. Instead something clicks on deep inside of us that turns us to the pragmatic. How can I fix this? becomes the sole question that captivates our hearts. Our first instinct is to hide and cover. These strategies passed down from our ancestors are most vividly on display in children who have had less time to refine and hone their dusty skill sets. My (Jamin) children hide when they do something wrong. Each child has distinct tactics, but the goal is the same. My daughter usually hides by doing something she thinks will please me. When she does something wrong, she will immediately offer to help clean up or ask if I want to color with her. My son's methods are more blatant. He runs away and buries his head in the couch so that I cannot see his face. Both techniques have their strengths and weaknesses, but both are ways of hiding from Dad. They are both attempting to hide the fact that they have sinned. They fear exposure.

Things are vastly different when I am playing hide-and-seek with my kids. They love to play hide-and-seek with me, but they are terrible at it. I am usually assigned the job of seeker, which is never very challenging. I hardly have the chance to ask the question "Where are you?" before they answer. Within a few seconds of looking, my kids will, without fail, jump out and expose their hiding places. "Here we are," they both yell in unison. My kids believe the real essence and joy of the game is in being found, not in hiding. They desire the moment Dad sees them and scoops them into his arms.

As a dad, these contrasting scenes tell me a great deal about my kids. Their postures toward me when we are playing hide-and-seek are completely contrary to their postures toward me in their sin. When we are playing hide-and-seek, my kids have a posture of exposure and embrace. Even when they are hiding, they are itching to reveal their positions, to be found, hugged, and laughed with. On the other hand, after doing something wrong, they often have a posture of fear, shame, and avoidance. They don't want to be seen. My job as a dad is to ask the same question I do when we are playing hide-and-seek: "Where are you?" My job is to call them out of hiding and to love them in the reality of their sin.

"Where are you?" That is *the question*. It was the first question God ever asked humanity. It is the question God asked Adam and Eve in the garden when they chose to hide from him. Much like me with my children, it came in a moment of sin. In fact, it was *the moment* of sin. Adam and Eve had chosen the way of dustiness and had become lost in their rebellion. God was aware of where Adam and Eve were. God was not bad at hide-and-seek. Rather, his question was an invitation to Adam and Eve.

God invites us to come out of hiding.

God invites us to reveal our dusty ways.

God invites us to himself.

We have moments throughout our lives when God invites us to come out of hiding. As I (Kyle) think back on several of these moments in my own life, I can still feel the emotional texture of exposure, the inner desire to hide and cover. My junior year of high school I was driving back from a favorite burger joint after an off-campus lunch. A friend of mine sat in the passenger seat as we drove with the windows down and music blaring. He thought it would be funny to throw jelly beans out the window at various cars and joggers. To our delight, he nailed a car's roof with five beans from a good fifteen yards. We were enjoying ourselves until the car tried to run us off the road. With much anxiety and fear, I slammed on my brakes as he skidded in front of me. I clipped the back end of his car as I fled the accident. Back at school in my next class, my heart raced and I quickly pondered all my options. Did he catch my license plate? Was there damage to his car? To my car? What story could I tell that would explain the damage? I could just say I found my car that way after school—accidents often happen in parking lots. As I tried my best to think my way out of it, the police showed up looking for me. I couldn't sink low enough in my chair. There was no explanation that would make the scenario go away. I was uncovered. Years later, I still think back and shudder, wishing I hadn't said what I did or had made different choices. Events long lost in the past are still present in my mind like beacons of guilt and shame, pronouncing judgment against me.

My experience of guilt and shame in sin is hardly unique. After Jesus' resurrection, we are told that he appeared to several of his disciples who were fishing. When Peter realized it was Jesus, he dove into the sea to swim to shore in order to see him (John 21:7). After eating breakfast, Jesus asked Peter three times if he loved him (John 21:15–19). The three inquiries no doubt correlated to Peter's threefold rejection of Jesus the night he was betrayed and arrested. That was no coincidence. Peter recognized the connection, and he was grieved (John 21:17).

Jesus didn't simply allow Peter's sin to be hidden in the past; he called it out with a voice of loving invitation.

Jesus opens the way to forgiveness and reconciliation, but not without pulling us into the reality of our sin. His light of grace pours forth, and its warmth is felt most strongly in the darkest places of sin. In a truly mysterious way, hope is found right in the midst of exposure. In contrast, the way of dustiness that is fixated on hiding from God is a place of hopelessness. There is no redemption there. Our strategies for hiding from God make redemption impossible, because by nature they deny the very presence of the only One who can redeem us.

Redemption follows honesty. Redemption always comes alongside humility, because redemption is a journey into the truth of who God is and who we are in relation to him. Redemption comes as we respond to God's question "Where are you?" by saying, "Here I am, Lord." Just as Peter had to receive the Lord's forgiveness within the story of his sin, so, too, must we proclaim, "Lord, you know everything; you know that I love you," from the midst of our own stories of sin (John 21:17).

Clothed by God

For many of us, the idea of being truly known—in all our sin—is horrifying. We have spent too many years trying to convince the world around us that we are not saturated with lust, anger, and greed. We create false identities of humility to hide our pride, and we end up generating a personality we think will thrive in church life even though we know it is a lie. Like Adam and Eve, when these realities are exposed, we try to brush them off by blaming someone or something else. Adam's response to God's unveiling question was to point the finger and avoid responsibility: "The woman whom you gave to be with me, she gave me fruit of the tree" (Gen. 3:12). Surely the problem was either the woman or God who made the woman! If he couldn't hide behind a fig leaf, perhaps his wife would work.

Only after the Lord explained the extent of the ruin Adam and Eve's sin would cause—how their relationships with God, each other, and creation were altered—did the Lord clothe them (Gen. 3:21). This action was pure mercy. After illuminating the demise of their relationships, God addressed what had become the greatest obstacle to relationship: their nakedness and their newfound sight. Their nakedness was shameful, so they had to live in constant hiding. By providing clothes, God did not take away their guilt, but he provided space to relate even in the midst of their brokenness and exposure. They can now engage in relationship without shame, because they can be known even as their nakedness is now covered. The eternal, infinite Creator of the universe continues to move in grace.

Christians have long noted that being clothed in this manner foreshadows the work of Christ to clothe his followers with his own righteousness. This is called alien righteousness because it is not something believers grasp as their own, but something they receive by grace. It is solely a gift. Grace is not earned, created, or owned, but is only received and embraced. Likewise, in the Genesis narrative, Adam and Eve received what they did not deserve as a gift from God. Unlike Christ's righteousness, these clothes did not put them in right standing;

but like Christ's righteousness, it provided the space for right relating.

Clothing people who are careening toward death might seem equivalent to setting up a string quartet as the Titanic descends to its watery grave. But to God, relationship is the highest priority. By giving them clothes, God created space for them to be human—to relate with each other and God—and therefore to know true life before death. He carved out a gracious place for their survival, a time set apart for his use. Sin may have entered creation, but God always sanctifies a space that he calls his creatures into. That sanctified space is God's own life, known first through God's people and physically through his temple, but known in its perfection in Christ. Just as creation was originally meant to be the temple of God's presence, so God is redeeming reality so that his presence will permeate all.

When I (Jamin) was a child, my dad would say, "You are the greatest boy in the world." As I got older, I began to see my limitations and my inadequacies, which caused me to question the truth of my dad's words. One evening I finally asked, "Why?" My dad recently admitted to me that the question put him on his heels a bit. "Why am I the greatest boy in the world?" After a moment of consideration he responded, "Because you are my son." He did not list my good qualities or my talents; in that moment my value was based on nothing more than the fact that I was his son. He had created me. I was his. Therefore, I was the most precious thing in the world to him.

Similarly, even before Adam and Eve dove into dustiness, they were reminded that they were valuable because God, their Maker, said so. Value was known through the eye of the beholder, just as my father praised me because I was his beloved son, not because of something I did. Only as we are beheld as valuable by God can we come to know our true value. Love humanized the creatures made from dust, just as sin went on to dehumanize them. God's clothing of his creatures points to a deeper plan to re-humanize his people through his love. God did not give up on his initial plan, nor was he surprised by sin. God created and clothed his creatures with an eye to their ultimate clothing—when they would be seen anew in Christ, beheld and humanized as one with *the* human, Christ.

Therefore, our humble human nature leaves us in a state of humiliation, which might seem overwhelming. However, God has carved out space for us in his own life. God has gifted himself to his creation by sending his Son and Spirit. This space is received in salvation and endowed as a gift by God. This space makes life with God possible. God does not offer forgiveness from a distance, nor does he want to set up a moral obstacle course for you to run so that he might accept you. God offers himself because he wants to live life with you. The Christian life is being with the God who is always with you, and therefore it entails a full reception of *who* you are. Just like Jamin and his dad, we must hear from our Father in heaven that we are valued because we are loved by him and clothed with Christ. We must hear from God that we are beloved. We must embrace our belovedness in the midst of our sins, our desire to make ourselves valuable, and our belief that we can generate a meaningful life on our own. *We must hear in the depths of our dusty souls that we are loved*, that it was while we were still sinners that he died for us (Rom. 5:8).

Worldly Strategies

Even though we have been clothed in Christ and called valuable, we are still tempted to believe our value is up to us. The idea that our value is from without, that it is in the eye of God's beholding, feels too uncertain, too distant, too out of our control. In our foolishness, we believe the things of this world are certain. We believe we can create unshakable foundations upon which to construct our value, all the while neglecting that Christ is the only solid rock on which to build. We seek out ways to secure our value in temporal things, rather than to know our value in light of eternal truth. As we do so, prayer makes less and less sense. As we adopt the values of the world, prayer seems pointless. Rather than focusing on the God who has called us to himself, our minds are caught up with questions about why prayer matters at all. Does it even do anything? We become so focused on getting life the way we want that being with God doesn't seem all that important.

Education was always valued in my family, but I (Kyle) was never much of a student. All the way through high school, I skated by without really applying myself. I just didn't care. Reality finally struck me shortly after high school. I was not going to become a professional athlete, to the surprise of no one but myself. I started to feel anxious about my future. *What would I do for a living? How would I make money?* I remember a distinct moment when I resorted to grasping at what would not fade away. *What could I do that couldn't be taken away from me?* I even thought to myself: *What could I hold on to even if I ended up homeless?* At that moment, I didn't grasp for Christ, but education. *If I had a master's or a doctorate*, I thought, *I could secure my value regardless of my circumstances.* I didn't turn to dependence, but to seeking my independence. I didn't turn to abiding in Christ, but to self-fulfillment. I didn't embrace the way of beloved dust, but succumbed to the way of dustiness.

Our attempts to self-fulfill work themselves out in our lives in the subtlest ways. We feel anxiety, so we shop. Life is frustrating or disappointing, so we become addicted to food, television, alcohol, drugs, etc. We feel undervalued, so we try to use other people and sex to make something of ourselves. We are insecure in our identities, so we build careers for all to see. We always feel beneath others, so we flaunt our money to try and prove we are valuable. Instead of holding these sinful inclinations up to the Lord in prayer, we turn to worldly things to try and appease our desires. These "solutions" offer no real help, but only cause more unrest in our soul. The only real solution is to come before the God of love in the midst of this brokenness.

Rest or Escape?

After nearly a decade of life with my chinchilla, the vet told us that he would have to be put down. Dusty was not doing so well. "Should we still allow him a final dust bath?" I asked the vet.

"Hmm," the vet pondered. "It probably isn't the best thing for him. But sure, let him. I would hate to take away the one thing that brings him so much joy."

Dustiness, in many ways, serves the same role in our lives. We grasp on to the base things of the world—the things below—in an attempt to find some vestige of comfort. Rather than finding freedom in the way of life God provided in his Son, we wander blindly in the way of death. Rather than entering the rest of God, initiated on the seventh day of creation, we anxiously search for rest anyplace else. We seek an escape into some mythical land of peace in order to avoid the harsh realities of our dusty world. Yet our self-generated place of rest is really *restless wandering*. Much like Adam and Eve's scramble to hide (Gen. 3:8), Cain's wandering (Gen. 4:14), and the people of Babel's scattering (Gen. 11:8), the way of dustiness in our lives is ultimately marked by restlessness, instability, and insecurity. We frantically seek to ground our lives and identities in something other than God. Rest, true rest, is always grounded in *relationship* and oriented in *reality*. In contrast, escape is grounded in *isolation* and oriented in *fantasy*. When we rest, we enter into relationship with God, and we cling to him in the truth of our dustiness. Rest and escape are diametrically opposed. Being dusty is living according to the strategies you have subconsciously developed to escape the reality of this broken world. It is the way of restlessness. Adopting this way means alienation from the life of God, the life that God offers to us in Christ.

Prayer As a Tool of Our Flesh

One telltale sign of the way of dustiness is the attempt to make the personal God of Scripture an object rather than the subject. Likewise, the way of dustiness always makes God a problem to solve rather than a personal God to engage with honestly. When you are confronted by God, is that a problem that needs to be solved by being better, acting appropriately, or saying the right thing? Or, when you are confronted by God, are you able to be known and loved? The way of dustiness seeks to hide rather than be exposed. The way of life seeks exposure before God, to grasp fully all that he has done for us. To know this way of life is to pray. But the dustiness within us runs so deep that even prayer itself succumbs to its seduction.

We live out the reality of our brokenness, the drive of our dustiness, in prayer. When a prayer is little more than rattling off all the things you did that you shouldn't have, that is not coming before the Lord of mercy and casting yourself at the foot of the cross, but is an attempt to deal with your guilt. Instead of proclaiming "Here I am" in honesty and vulnerability, our response to the Lord tends to be, "Here is what I think you want from me, so please take it and go." Like Adam and Eve peering through the bushes, we hope we can use prayer (or church, giving, good works) to our advantage and not deal with the messiness of relating to God on his own terms. Prayer becomes another way to dominate life, to have a leg up to secure the life we want. In prayer we come to the crucified One and demand a way of life void of the cross. Prayer becomes a tool of our flesh rather than the submission of our flesh before the penetrating gaze of God (Heb. 4:12–13).

Likewise, instead of being known in prayer, we try to be good.[2] Rather than receiving God's love and acceptance as the grounding of our identity, prayer becomes a place to make God love us. For many, prayer is the solution to their unbelief and inability to accept that they *have already been* received in love. Prayer becomes a place to prove to God that we are trying as hard as we can. This is the death of prayer. Because we tend to think of prayer as a pure, spiritual activity, it is often the place where our vice and depravity reign without notice. In fact, prayer could be the most fleshly activity we engage in. In prayer we often hide from God by projecting our strategies to avoid his penetrating gaze. This can occur any number of ways, not the least by solely focusing on praying for others. An activity that seems so selfless can fuel selfishness and an attempt to "right yourself" with God. Prayer is a place to receive. Prayer is a place to be known. Prayer is not a place to escape reality, but is a place to rest with God in reality.

In light of this, it is important to open our hearts to some questions concerning our prayer lives. Like David's sin with Bathsheba, which kept on growing and growing with every attempt to cover it up, do your prayers attempt to hide your tracks? In other words, when you pray, do you try to appease God so that your sin won't come back to haunt you? Have you turned prayer into a "robber's den," the place where you go and hide and hope not to get caught (Matt. 21:13)? Or, rather, is prayer the place where your dustiness is made known? Is prayer a place to find hope and righteousness, not in yourself but in Christ, and to learn to rest in him rather than in your own accomplishments (or lack thereof)? Just as God clothed Adam and Eve to create space for relationship, do you also receive Christ's righteousness and rest in him, or do you try to cover yourself with your own righteousness? Is prayer often lost in your life because you attempt to generate spiritual growth apart from relating with God personally? Or, on the other hand, do you want relationship with God but hope to avoid the messiness of law, sin, and the cross? This is what worldly spirituality offers in spades. Does your prayer life reveal that you want to be *spiritual* but not a Christian? Do you want the benefits of life with God on your own terms, without having to trust in God's plan for what that entails?

Grace is not simply God turning his head away from our sin, nor is it God's niceness. Grace is God opening up his life to us in Christ. In prayer this means that we have access to the Father through Christ, as we have the Spirit abiding in us (Eph. 2:18). This is our space for prayer. We have been clothed with Christ, and have therefore died and been raised with him, so we can stand before God as his own. Many Christians never pray from this place. Rather, we try to construct our own safe places for prayer, such as creating the identity of someone who is mature (or at least looks mature). Or, it could be that our safe place before God is believing we are "good people." Whatever it is, it is foreign and hostile to true prayer.

Prayer is the place to come out of hiding. "Prayer is not the place to be good, but the place to be honest."[3] How honest are your prayers? Likewise, prayer is not the place to escape, but to know rest. Prayer is not the place to hide, but to abide. Is being with God your respite, or do you try to use him to avoid dealing with your life, sin, and pain? In calling us to himself, God calls us as we are. God's call is often "Where are you?" or even, "Do you love me?" And it is not a one-time question but a continual call to our hearts. The response he seeks is for us to come to him as we are rather than frantically looking for ways to hide the truth of our hearts.

We are all left to answer these questions for ourselves: Will we turn to rest or escape? Will we be God's beloved dust, or will we embrace dustiness? Will we receive the clothes of Christ's righteousness or try to weave our own? In Jesus' ministry, he encountered large numbers of people who, when confronted with the truth of themselves and God, either suppressed the truth by avoiding him or else strategized ways to kill him. This is the posture of the human heart. Like it or not, you have a heart that wants to writhe around in dustiness when God offers you glory. When God calls you to himself, will you position yourself as a servant or a far-off admirer? When God draws you to himself in love, will you come up with ways to turn the relationship into a business transaction? When God called Adam and Eve out into the open and clothed them, he was creating space for them to be with him. In Christ, God has advanced this plan exponentially. In Christ we are clothed, known, and received in love. We are called beloved because we are his own. It is in this place that we can pray in honesty, learning to live all of life with God as he is with us.

FIVE

I AM DUST: NOW
EVERYTHING CHANGES //

HE WAS HARD at work. Still out in the fields in the waning hours of the workday, he was busy directing the servants' activities. Then, suddenly, he heard music in the distance. *Where could that be coming from?* he wondered, as he quickly called for a servant to explain. The servant responded, "Your brother has come, and your father has killed the fattened calf, because he has received him back safe and sound" (Luke 15:27). This is the older brother of the prodigal son, the brother who is often ignored by readers of Jesus' parable. This brother never left home. This brother did not demand his inheritance. This brother did not throw away the family money on foolishness and sin. Rather, this brother was hardworking. This brother was a man of good character. This brother stood by his father and watched his younger brother break their father's heart and leave.

Jesus told this parable in response to the Pharisees' and scribes' grumblings about how he received and ate with sinners

(Luke 15:2). In the parable, the older brother was the Pharisee. He was the one who looked like his father only on the outside, while inside he was broken. He was the one who had done all he was supposed to do, and yet his heart was filled with anger. Whereas the father in the parable was filled with mercy upon seeing the younger son return, the older brother was filled with anger, showing how little he had in common with the father. The older son, no doubt, thought he was being faithful, just as the Pharisees did. He believed he was fulfilling his duty to be good. But that was the problem. The younger son came back humbled and offered himself as a servant. The father refused to receive him as such, and instead embraced him as a son. The older son never left home, but he did not come to the father in humility. The older son never sold his identity as a child, but he became a servant in his heart. He had not embraced his sonship. When his father pursued him, he declared, "Look, these many years I have served you, and I never disobeyed your command" (Luke 15:29). He had not left home, but his heart had. The tragedy of the story is not a son leaving home and returning as a servant—the real tragedy is the son who stayed at home and somehow lost his identity anyway.

The heart of this story is the Father's response to his oldest: "Son, you are always with me, and all that is mine is yours" (Luke 15:31). The older son had failed to realize that his true identity was found within the life of the father—being *with* his father. He had tried to be dutiful to make his life what he wanted it to be, rather than receiving the life of the father as the foundation for his obedience. He was trying to create an identity rather than allowing the father to speak his true identity over him. He never embraced himself as a son, and therefore, like so many of us, he became dutiful for God as his heart slowly died.

The younger son, in contrast to the older, could be embraced as a child of the father because he came to him with nothing but himself. He was able to rest on the grace of the father's self-giving. What else could he rest on? All the money was gone, and with it, his identity within the family. He had nothing and was scraping by, feeding pigs. He returned home as a servant and was totally undone and completely unveiled. Even his older brother knew that he had blown the family money on prostitutes (Luke 15:30). Like Adam and Eve who found themselves naked and ashamed, needing clothing to be with God and each other, so, too, did the younger son need to be covered. The father in the parable threw the family robe around his shoulders and put the family rings on his fingers, welcoming him back into fellowship with himself. The father famously said, "my son was dead, and is alive again; he was lost, and is found" (Luke 15:24).

In the parable, the father remained at home when his younger son left, and when the younger son returned, he was overflowing with mercy. But our Father in heaven is different. Our Father in heaven has a Son—a Son sent to the "far country," just like the younger son in the parable.[1] This Son was not disobedient. This Son didn't demand the inheritance. This Son didn't spend money foolishly. Rather, this Son journeyed forth propelled by the mercy of the Father. Like the father who ran to embrace his wayward son, this Son, Jesus, descended into our very nature. This is a "far country" filled with reckless living, even if it is not his reckless living. Just like the father who wrapped the robes of the family around the shoulders of his lost child, Jesus took on our nature—clothing himself with our brokenness—so that he could throw the robes of the Father around the shoulders of his children. In the incarnation we see a God who didn't wait, but who ran into the brokenness of his children.

We have seen that we are dust and that our lives are dusty. Likewise, we have seen that our dustiness leads us to reject God's presence for our own power and abilities. In Jesus we see God's response. Here, we turn our attention to the One who took on dust and dwelt among us—Jesus. This is the unforeseen twist in the plot that changed everything. In the divine drama, Jesus absorbed the brokenness of the first half of the story and relived it in his own life. Jesus retold the drama through himself, and therefore changed the ending. Because of sin, the consequence of death seemed inevitable, but Jesus walked through death to break open a new possibility beyond death. To understand the nature of the Christian life as God with us, we have to understand Christ. To understand what happens when we pray, we must attend to the work of Christ.

The Word Became Dust

The incarnation was earth shattering. The One who created the universe stepped into creation itself: "The Word became flesh and dwelt among us, and we have seen his glory, glory as of the only Son from the Father, full of grace and truth" (John 1:14). The infinite and eternal God willingly took on a finite and temporal existence. More provocatively, he didn't take on a body of power and authority; instead, we encounter God in a manger in the form of a weak and needy infant. A new act in the drama is being written of rescue, redemption, and restoration. In the first act, beloved dust was lost, but in this story it is found. Jesus became beloved dust and invited us to life in him—the life of the beloved.

God the Creator does not have a history, but we creatures do. We are bound by time, and God is eternal. By becoming fully human, he took on our temporality and finitude. Jesus had a history. Adam's family tree was a long history of dustiness, and Jesus entered that dustiness to redeem it from the inside out. He came to rewrite history. A history of rebellion, faithlessness, and sin was coming to an end; a new history of trust, faithfulness, and righteousness was breaking forth. Behold, the old was going, and the new was coming. The history under Adam was a dehumanized story—a story of dustiness. The history under the new Adam (Jesus Christ) would be a fully human story—a story of dust being embraced as beloved.

One of the more subtle aspects of Jesus' life and ministry was his taking the stories of Israel and retelling them through his own life. Whether it was Israel's forty years of wandering in the wilderness, the exodus, the temple, or even the garden, Jesus pulled the stories into his life and retold them in a new light. But it wasn't just a simple retelling, as if he merely wanted to be an itinerant storyteller. Rather, Jesus was redeeming Israel's life and history through creative reimagining. We can find our own broken histories caught up in his life, death, resurrection, and ascension, now redeemed and retold through his continued ministry. For prayer, this means that Jesus' redeeming and retelling of our lives with God must reorient our posture before him. More specifically, Jesus reorients our prayers. Jesus' prayers become our own prayers, and our prayers find their way to God in Christ.

It is this retelling that we are invited to participate in, and as we do so, we get to participate in the redemption of our brokenness. We are invited to share in the new temple, the new exodus, and the new creation. He invites us to share in the new family tree, to be born again as beloved sons and daughters. In the incarnation he invites us to be grafted into the tree of life. He invites us to be truly human, to embrace our createdness fully as he has already embraced it. Rather than participating in the history of Adam, we now participate in the history of Jesus. Rather than participating in original sin, we now participate in Christ's righteousness. As Christians, this is our new history. We are always marked by our first history, but it is the new history that *truly* defines our identity and future as beloved dust.

Not by Magic

Every now and again, in movies or TV shows, a character will pray. Often the character has shown no previous interest in God. Usually fueled by some tragic circumstance, the character will beg the God he or she doesn't believe in for something, sometimes anything. This is often accompanied by promises that will never be kept, such as being a better person or giving more money away. These prayers are often to a God far off and removed, showing little to no interest in the day-to-day workings of the world. This God's existence and relevance, it is assumed, are not important for the mundane realities of life. This God mimics the genie in the bottle who can be called, when needed, to make your life better.

Thankfully, Christian prayer moves much deeper and offers much more than this. For one thing, God is not our magic genie. Much more importantly, God is not some transcendent deity who may or may not engage in the world. He is the God who gave himself to his creation in Christ Jesus. Jesus changes everything about our posture before God. The question we have to ask here is, how? What is it about who Jesus is and what he has done that changes prayer? We will build on this for the remainder of the book as we see how prayer changes because of who Christ is for us.

It is true that God sometimes answers the prayers of desperation just mentioned. But ultimately, the reason Christians don't pray this way is because we know God. God is not some transcendent power or force; he is the personal God who has revealed himself to us in Jesus. "God" is not a name we give an unknown deity; he is Father, Son, and Holy Spirit. This profound reality unearths something equally profound—our prayers trace along the contours of who God is and what he has done. In other words, our prayers do not echo into the darkness of eternity hoping to be heard by an unknown God. Rather, our prayers follow a specific trajectory to God's heart because of what Christ has done for us. The way we learn to pray is to listen intently to God's self-revelation, and the trajectory to God's heart becomes clear. We learn to pray as we focus on Jesus.

God's Word became dust and dwelt among us. This is the provocative and counterintuitive reality of the gospel. God became what we are that we might share in his life of love. God took on our humanity and brokenness—both our dust and our dustiness—and sanctified it for himself. Christ stood in our stead, doing what we had always failed to do, and lived a life of faithful obedience to the Father in the Spirit. John started his gospel with the revolutionary claim that "the Word became flesh and dwelt among us" (John 1:14). But that translation does not reach the depths of how provocative of a claim that is. Rather, "the Word became flesh, and *tabernacled* among us, and we beheld His glory."[2] The Word of God became a new temple among us. In Jesus, the purpose of creation as the temple of God's presence was once again perceived. Just as the original temple revealed the *shekinah* glory of God (2 Chron. 7:1–3), so Jesus came as a new temple, and in a new way revealed God's glory to his people.

The New Temple

We have already seen that creation was God's cosmic temple, the place God revealed his presence. Within that temple was a place of God's specific and relational presence: the garden of Eden. After sin broke humankind's relationship with God, God created a means to be relationally present with his people. He had them build a temple. The physical temple was the place where heaven and earth met. It was the localized presence of God with his people. Like the parable of the two sons, the temple was God's running to his people and clothing them (this "clothing" was the sacrificial system). God physically carved out space to be with them, and he created the context by which people could come to him forgiven, redeemed, and beloved. As the locus of God's presence with his creation, the temple was the center of the world. The Jewish view of the world told them that heaven and earth were not two isolated realms, but that they actually "overlap[ped] and interlock[ed]" in the temple.[3] The truth of God's cosmic temple served as a pattern for the physical temple (Heb. 8:1–5). Jesus redefined that reality around himself.

As the center of the world, the temple was also the center of Jewish identity. It grounded their firm devotion to the land that the Lord had given them, and it was a visual reminder that the Lord would never leave them. The land wasn't a side issue for the Israelites, but was ingrained in their relationship with God from the beginning. For instance, Jacob had a dream where there was a ladder set upon the earth with its top reaching to heaven. Angels ascended and descended on the ladder, showing it to be where heaven and earth met (Gen. 28:10–12). Fulfilling this, Jesus told Nathanael, "Truly, truly, I say to you, you will see heaven opened, and the angels of God ascending and descending on the Son of Man" (John 1:51). The "Son of Man," Jesus, was the ladder revealed to Jacob in his dream. Jesus was the *place* where heaven and earth met. Jesus was the land and the temple that would serve as a light to the nations, blessing every family on earth. The church's call to be *in* Christ is an invitation to participate with him in that blessing. Now, spread throughout the world, the people of God mediate his presence to the world as bricks built on the cornerstone of the new temple, Christ. Rather than following Babel, where we assemble bricks into a tower to reach God, God has come down as the cornerstone of the new temple, and he forms us into a temple of his presence for the world.

To understand the life of prayer, one must first understand that God's presence has been broken open to us in Christ and the Spirit. In Christ, we are ushered into a new temple, and therefore it is within that new temple that we pray to the Father.

All our prayers are prayed *in Christ* (John 16:26–27). Our prayers often fail right where our attempts to save ourselves do, in the act of trying to achieve the impossible. We are not called to self-generate righteousness any more than we are called to self-generate prayer. God gives us his presence and gives us his righteousness. We are to receive him as he gives himself, and respond in the truth of who we are. When we self-generate prayer, we seek to pray *well* instead of praying in truth. Rather, we are called to the Father, in the Son, by the Holy Spirit—to be with God as he really is.

Something Greater

I (Kyle) remember getting a passport for the first time. I was going on an overseas mission trip, and I was excited to get some stamps in that little book that was far too clean and crisp. A good passport is a well-worn one. I wasn't interested in getting a passport to lay in my desk drawer or to hide under my socks. It was the key to the world, so why would someone bother to get a key and not unlock the door?

Unfortunately many of us have passports sitting locked securely away without any use. Not actual passports, but the passport given to us by God. In taking on our condition, Jesus gave us "access" to the Father (Eph. 2:18). In Christ we are given access to the life of God, and yet, many people refuse to embrace that access to see and know the world. Many people hide it away as if the treasure is found simply in having it. Like the older son in the parable of the two sons, simply accepting the name son became good enough, even if he did not know himself as a child

of the Father. When the Father sought him out and called him
to be with the family, the older son refused. Even when he heard
the words, "Son, you are always with me, and all that is mine is
yours" (Luke 15:31), he did not enter in to the life of the family.

Jesus proclaimed to the Pharisees that "something greater
than the temple is here" (Matt. 12:6). Jesus was greater because
God's presence was revealed in him more fully and more completely than before. As the new temple, the greater temple, Jesus
went around fulfilling the role of the temple outside (and even
inside) its walls. He forgave people of their sins (Luke 7:49–
50), something God did previously through the temple alone.
Furthermore, the temple was the place of God's rest (Ps. 132).
As the Lord reigned through his temple, it was a place of rest for
his people as well.[4] Jesus also took over that aspect of the temple,
reigning in his kingdom and providing rest in himself:

> All things have been handed over to me by my Father, and
> no one knows the Son except the Father, and no one knows
> the Father except the Son and anyone to whom the Son
> chooses to reveal him. Come to me, all who labor and are
> heavy laden, and I will give you rest. Take my yoke upon you,
> and learn from me, for I am gentle and lowly in heart, and
> you will find rest for your souls. (Matt. 11:27–29)

When Jesus died, the veil in the temple was torn in two,
symbolizing that the separation between people and God was
abolished in Christ (Matt. 27:51). God's presence was made
available to the world in the sacrifice of Christ.

When Jesus "cleansed" the temple, flipping over the tables

of the money-changers and the seats of those selling sacrifices (Mark 11:15–19), he explained his actions by saying, "My house shall be called a house of prayer," quoting Isaiah 56:7. Isaiah 56 outlines that God desires all people, foreigners, and eunuchs (those cut off from God by the temple) to come to him in prayer: "My house shall be called a house of prayer for all peoples" (Isa. 56:7). Jesus became that house of prayer.

Right after Jesus condemned the temple for ceasing to be a house of prayer for the world, "the blind and the lame came to him in the temple, and he healed them" (Matt. 21:14). Within the temple's walls were people cut off from God's presence because of their brokenness. Jesus healed them. But Jesus was doing much more than healing. He was reestablishing the way the world worked. Jesus was breaking open a way to be in the presence of God that did not draw the boundaries the temple so quickly drew. Jesus healed them, yes, but the bigger picture was that Jesus was healing the world. As Jesus enacted the true meaning of the temple, children praised him (Matt. 21:15–16). Within this passage we see prayer, healing, awe, and praise, all features of life in the temple. Now these are refocused around Jesus. He was the new temple; in him we know true prayer and ultimate healing, and he is the proper object of our awe and praise. He took on dust; therefore it was to him that dust had to go to be with God. As summarized by N. T. Wright:

> Heaven and earth were being joined up—but no longer in the temple in Jerusalem. The joining place was visible where the healings were taking place, where the party was going on (remember the angels celebrating in heaven and people

joining in on earth?), where forgiveness was happening. In other words, the joining place, the overlapping circle, was taking place where Jesus was and in what he was doing. Jesus was, as it were, a walking temple. A living, breathing place-where-Israel's-God-was-living.[5]

God's presence was no longer wrapped up in a temple building, but was offered in a new kind of temple—the body of Christ. In the Spirit, the body was opened up to people of all nations to partake in the glory of the Lord. We are now a part of this presence as the Spirit indwells us and unites us to Christ. God is *for us* in the incarnation in a way never before seen. God ties himself to his creation and plan of redemption. God reveals himself to the world as the suffering servant. God does not send armies of angels to punish the evildoers in his creation, but sends the Lamb of God to take away the sins of the world.

The Son of Heaven and Dust

The older I (Kyle) become, the more identities I take on. I am a son, brother, husband, dad, uncle, cousin, professor, author, and the list could easily go on. While we all have various identities, some are more fundamental than others. We find the same to be true with Jesus. Jesus was a prophet. Jesus was a priest. Jesus was king. He was all these things, but none of them are the bedrock of his identity. Similarly, as we've seen, Jesus was the new temple. These are roles Jesus played and continues to play, but they are not fundamentally *who* Jesus is. Jesus *is* the Son. Above all else, Jesus is *the* Son of the Father.

The author of the letter to the Hebrews started his missive with the bold claim that "long ago, at many times and in many ways, God spoke to our fathers by the prophets, but in these last days he has spoken to us by his Son" (Heb. 1:1–2). He went on to say, concerning the Son, "Your throne, O God, is forever and ever" and, "You, Lord, laid the foundation of the earth in the beginning, and the heavens are the work of your hands" (Heb. 1:8, 10). Jesus was no normal messenger sent by God to relay his guidance. He was God's Son. This Son, true and eternal God with the Father and the Spirit, took on humanity in his person— being born, growing, suffering, and dying at the hands of those he came to save. This Son opened the way of life because he was life himself (John 14:6). He took humanity on in his person to do what humanity had always failed to do, to be faithful (2 Tim. 2:13). In him we have a redeemer, a savior, and a brother:

> Therefore he had to be made like his brothers in every respect, so that he might become a merciful and faithful high priest in the service of God, to make propitiation for the sins of the people. For because he himself has suffered when tempted, he is able to help those who are being tempted. (Heb. 2:17–18)

It's a Family Matter

Jesus opened up the life of the Father in his own life that we, too, can partake in God's life as children. In other words, God the Father sent the Son because salvation entails adoption. Look at Paul's depiction of this reality:

But when the fullness of time had come, God sent forth his Son, born of woman, born under the law, to redeem those who were under the law, so that we might receive adoption as sons and daughters. And because you are sons and daughters, God has sent the Spirit of his Son into our hearts, crying, "Abba! Father!" So you are no longer a slave, but a son or daughter, and if a son or daughter, then an heir through God. (Gal. 4:4–7)[6]

Salvation is a family issue, so God sent his Son. We can often neglect this reality and try to make salvation simply a legal issue, as if our relationship with God is forged in the courtroom alone. This unfortunately reduces the gospel so much that it loses its vitality. It is a move to make it more palatable, more understandable. Rather, the provocative reality of the gospel is that in Christ's Sonship we become sons and daughters of God. It is not in a courtroom, but in a family where we come to know ourselves as children of God. The Son of God took on dust and was faithful in our place so that we, too, could be children of God. God sent forth his Son because he was not simply dealing with legal issues—he was dealing with family issues. God did not send the Son only for forgiveness; he sent the Son so that we could truly partake of the life of love shared between the Father, the Son, and the Holy Spirit.

In Romans we find this same picture. The central features of the gospel are irreducibly personal: the Father sending the Son who sends the Spirit. Paul started out talking about the law:

There is therefore now no condemnation for those who are *in Christ Jesus*. For the law of the *Spirit of life* has set you free *in Christ Jesus* from the law of sin and death. For God has done what the law, weakened by the flesh, could not do. By sending *his own Son* in the likeness of sinful flesh and for sin, he condemned sin in the flesh, in order that the righteous requirement of the law might be fulfilled in us, who walk not according to the flesh but according *to the Spirit.* (Rom. 8:1–4, emphasis added)

In the midst of a discussion of law, we see the central features of redemption—Christ and the Spirit. To understand the gospel, we focus our attention on who God is in Christ and in the Spirit and what he does through them. As we are in Christ, we are set free from the law of sin and death, and as we have the Spirit, we put aside the deeds of the flesh. But what is the main focus here? Paul continued in verse 14:

For all who are led by the Spirit of God are sons or daughters of God. For you did not receive the spirit of slavery to fall back into fear, but you have received the Spirit of adoption as sons and daughters, by whom we cry, "Abba! Father!" The Spirit himself bears witness with our spirit that we are children of God, and if children, then heirs—heirs of God and fellow heirs with Christ . . . (Rom. 8:14–17)[7]

Here, we see that our identities are found from without, rather than from within. We receive our identities through the proclamation of God. You are a child. You are *God's* child. By receiving the Spirit of adoption you call out to God, "Abba! Father!" Grasping who you are in Christ is to pray. Receiving the Spirit is crying out "Abba! Father!" It is grasping that you are beloved of the Lord. Prayer flows forth from those who know themselves as God's, forgiven and redeemed in him. Knowing yourself in this manner is also knowing yourself in Christ, and therefore taking on his way of life in the world. His way of life is the way of a child, of one who "did not count equality with God a thing to be grasped, but emptied himself" (Phil. 2:6–7). Jesus embraced the dependent life of a child. This is the life we know in Christ. This leads us to a rich and robust praise of God's adopting grace found in Paul's letter to the Ephesians. Paul proclaimed,

> Blessed be the God and Father of our Lord Jesus Christ, who has blessed us in Christ with every spiritual blessing in the heavenly places, even as he chose us in him before the foundation of the world, that we should be holy and blameless before him. *In love he predestined us for adoption as sons through Jesus Christ*, according to the purpose of his will, to the praise of his glorious grace, with which he has blessed us in the Beloved. (1:3–6, emphasis added)

What Jesus had by nature we are offered by grace—sonship. Paul continued in Ephesians 2:18–19: "For through him we both have access in one Spirit to the Father. So then you are no longer strangers and aliens, but you are fellow citizens with the saints and members of the household of God." In receiving the Spirit we have access to the Father *through* the Son. This life known in Christ, the life in the Spirit as children before the Father, outlines the contours of our prayer. Just as we pray in Jesus' name, so we pray as those who share in his sonship. We pray *to* the Father, *in* the Son, *by* the Holy Spirit as those who have been caught up in God's own life. Therefore we seek the things that are above so that we can live in the way of Christ in this world. Notice Paul's description in Colossians 3: "If then you have been raised with Christ, seek the things that are above, where Christ is, seated at the right hand of God. Set your minds on things that are above, not on things that are on earth. For you have died, and your life is hidden with Christ in God" (vv. 1–3). The broad narrative of conversion is that God gave himself to us in the Son, and the Son who took on our nature has died and risen from the dead so that we have an entrance into God's own life. That entrance is the Son (the way, the truth, and the life), and we exist in him as he gives us his Spirit, the Spirit of life.

My (Jamin) son loves to collect rocks. We learned this on our first family vacation. We planned to spend most of the trip hiking and exploring. A few feet into our first trail, he had already stuffed so many rocks in his pockets that his pants were falling down. I noticed the slow descent of his trousers and the lumps in his pockets. I watched him as he continued to pick up rocks along the trail. I told him he couldn't pick up any more, and in fact he needed to dump the ones he had. It was an audacious suggestion. He refused. He treasured those rocks (most of which I discovered later were merely dirt clods). He finally did relinquish some of the earthen weights from his pockets, but doing so took a good deal of coaxing. It was odd to me to see his deep remorse in parting with dirt. He loved those dirt clods. They were his. They might not have been gold or amethyst, but they were beautiful and fantastic to my three-year-old. He wanted them. It was in his treasuring of them that they were made special, and consequently many of them made the car ride home. How could I demand that he leave behind what he loved so dearly? They had value because he valued them. They were beautiful because he cherished them.

We are beautiful because we are cherished by God. We are valuable because we are his. We come to embrace these realities in the Christian life by being with God. We come to know our value as beloved dust in prayer. Like those dirt clods that my son loved so much, we find ourselves in the hands of a God who is fantastically in love with us. From the beginning this was God's intention, to hold us, to cherish us—his beloved, image-bearing dust. We, finite and temporal creatures, are in desperate need of our loving Creator. We are formed to be with him in dependent, intimate, and abiding relationship. Yet humanity has chosen to pursue life outside of God, to look for a place of rest elsewhere. However, in Jesus Christ we are welcomed back to the place we belong. We are welcomed back into the hands of the Father as adopted children. We are welcomed to be with God who is always with us.

As believers we cannot understand *who* we are, and we certainly cannot understand the life of prayer, until we grasp that in Christ we are embraced by the Father. In the work of Christ we are united to him, such that his work is our work. Christ has pulled us into himself, so that his faith is our faith, his righteousness our righteousness, his prayers our prayers, and his sonship becomes our own. Christ has broken open the life of God within his own life and ministry. It is a life that is available by grace in the Spirit to those with faith. It is faith that allows us to "seek the things that are above, where Christ is, seated at the right hand of God," but we have to fully grasp the significance of who Christ is in relation to the Father (Col. 3:1). Christ's role as Son and temple come together in his role as priest. In Hebrews 8 we are told that "we have such a high priest, one who is seated at the right hand of the throne of the Majesty in heaven, a minister in the holy places, in the true tent that the Lord set up, not man" (vv. 1–2). Our lives are hidden with Christ in God. And Christ governs the temple of the Lord—not a physical temple, but an eternal, heavenly one. In Christ we have a High Priest who mediates for us, prays for us, and who calls us to the Father as his own children. In Christ, we are free to be with our Father and know ourselves as his children. As High Priest, Christ leads us before the Father; as the Son of God, he leads us before the Father as fellow children, as brothers and sisters with him, the true Son.

To Dust You Shall Return

God is the God of history. He has always been so. But even while he stands above history, he wielded his authority over history by entering into it. Jesus became a creature without ever ceasing to be the Creator. Jesus descended into our reality and sanctified it for himself. Jesus took on our brokenness and our destiny to break open God's destiny for humanity. God entered into the age of sin and death, taking them upon himself, and therefore defeating the powers of darkness.

The inevitability that we would return to dust echoed throughout time, until in the fullness of time Christ called out from the depth of dust itself: "It is finished!" (John 19:30). This call, from the condemnation of the cross, is a call of hope. It is a call that redeems and transforms our return to dust. Throughout time people have returned to dust in death. The ground has become the resting place for humanity as we breathe our last breaths. By Christ taking on our dust and dustiness, the return to dust changes. For believers, "to dust you shall return" is now a promise that we shall return to the one who has taken on dust—Christ Jesus—and know eternal life in him. As believers, the dust of death is not our destiny because dustiness has died in Christ's death. The God who took on dust descended into the grave of dust, and it could not hold him. "To dust you shall return" is now the victory cry of those who have died and been raised with the Son of God. Death has lost its victory and its sting (1 Cor. 15:55), and those who keep Christ's word will never see death (John 8:51). Christ became dust and has redeemed us from the oppressive cycle of death that looms inevitably on our horizon. Your life, your true life, is already hidden with Christ in God.

Therefore, our created destiny is revealed in Christ, that we, too, are children of God. As John made clear in his famous exposition, "For God so loved the world, that he gave his only Son, that whoever believes in him should not perish but have eternal life" (John 3:16). The person who believes in Christ "does not come into judgment, but has passed from death to life" (John 5:24). Baptism, we are told by Paul, represents the reality that in Christ's death we die, and therefore in Christ's resurrection we are raised to new life (Rom. 6-7). We have been "born from above" and can now live with Christ's life in us. As

Paul stated so explicitly, "It is no longer I who live, but Christ who lives in me. And the life I now live in the flesh I live by faith in the Son of God, who loved me and gave himself for me" (Gal. 2:20). Eternal life is the life given in Christ, and that life is lived as the way of love in the world. Eternal life is not simply a matter of length, but a matter of source. We have life in God, life abundant and true. We already live the eternal life, which is the life offered in Christ's resurrected life and given through the Spirit of life. And why is this life given? That we may live in his presence.

This is prayer: the texture of a life lived in the presence of God. In Christ's life, death, and resurrection we come to know what it means to be beloved dust. It is being caught up in God's movement to redeem a people to himself. It is being drawn in to the life of God, through Christ, by the Spirit, so that we can rest in Christ's love as children of the Father. It is living our days in the temple of God, with Christ as our High Priest, so that all of our existence, from church life to the most mundane tasks in our days, are now done in the presence of the God of love. It is here, in Christ, where we come to stand before the Father and receive his acceptance, mercy, and love, and therefore where our prayer completely changes tenor. It is here, *in* Christ, that we finally come to grasp what it means to be human. We have died, and now by grace, we can truly live. We are dust, and to dust we have returned—the dust taken up by Christ who has redeemed, sanctified, and glorified dust within himself. We now set our minds on Christ, and therefore pray in an entirely new way, now that our great High Priest eternally sits with the Father. Now, as believers in Christ, we are no longer "merely" human (1 Cor. 3:4), but are partakers of God's own life (2 Peter 1:4).

Abba! Father!

When Jesus was transfigured before Peter, James, and John, Moses and Elijah appeared. Luke told us that Jesus spoke to them about his coming *exodus*, even though it is often unhelpfully translated as "departure" (Luke 9:31). The word *departure* isn't all that significant, but for a Jewish reader, the word *exodus* is saturated with meaning. Jesus was focusing on his calling, which was a retelling (redeeming) of the exodus narrative. He was walking the way of the cross, which would lead him through the sea of death to ascend to the Father (rather than through the Red Sea and up Mt. Sinai, like Moses). Jesus ascended to the Father in our nature, and therefore in him we have access to the Father. In Christ and his redemption we can now call out, "Abba! Father!" This only happens in Christ. Our prayers, therefore, find their meaning in Christ. Our prayers have to follow the way of Christ because Christ is the sacred space of our standing before the Father.

Since prayer is being with God who is always with us, "being with" entails coming to the Father in the ascended Son. We may be dust, but we are adopted dust—dust given life, redemption, and salvation in the Son. We do not come before the Father on our own standing, but on Christ's. We do not come in our own name, but in Christ's. We do not have anything of our own as we stand before the Father; we come as Christ's. It is in that place that we are free, and there that we can love God and love our neighbors as ourselves, the true calling given to children of God.

Therefore, as we come in prayer, we come as those already justified before God. Even our prayers have been justified. Biblical theologian Graeme Goldsworthy put it well:

> As with every other aspect of our humanness in which we fall short of the glory of God, he provides for us the basis of full acceptance. In Christ we cannot be condemned as inadequate or "failed" prayerers. I should not think, because I don't pray as I ought, that God is less inclined to listen to me than he is to listen to some great prayer warrior.[8]

We come as those who have been accepted, not in our goodness, but in our sin. Just as in salvation, so, too, in prayer, we must come to God as we truly are. We come as those begging for eyes to see and ears to hear, as those who seek grace as the gift God provides. In prayer we must come as the needy, feeling the reality of sin; but prayer is also the place where we are rich, because we have already received Christ. To embrace the life of prayer, we must embrace Christ. He is the yes to our prayers, in whom we proclaim "Amen" (2 Cor. 1:20).

SIX

THE SONG OF THE BELOVED //

I (JAMIN) FACED a circle of blank stares. It was a standoff, and I was willing to wait. As a youth pastor, I had grown accustomed to this response from my students. I had asked a simple question: "Would anyone be willing to pray?" But as any youth pastor can tell you, it is not that simple. You would think I had asked the group of teenage boys if they had viewed pornography recently. Eventually, the same student that always broke the awkward silence prayed, if for no other reason than to alleviate the anxiety of his peers.

As a youth pastor, I encountered many difficult and disheartening moments, such as finding out a student lived a completely different lifestyle than I had known. However, as my tenure in youth ministry grew, those moments of cold sweat from my students became the saddest. The sadness only increased when I discovered that prayer was missing from their lives completely. My students simply had no idea what prayer was. For them, prayer was a duty and a ritual. It was not an invitation, but a requirement. It was not a time to be real, but a time to be presentable. Prayer had become a static, lifeless, and boring act. It had been sterilized. It had nothing to do with real life. It certainly wasn't personal or relational. Beyond the obligatory prayer before meals and possibly at bedtime, most of my students had never been taught or modeled a life of prayer. Sure, it occurred at church, but that was a religious setting. The professional Christian (the pastor) prayed, but that was his thing. Prayer was lofty and "spiritual"; it was something you were supposed to do, but my students didn't really know why.

This vacuum of prayer is another sign of the moralism that has eviscerated what life in God is all about. Prayer is another thing to check off the list of Christian activity, and it's pretty low on the list because prayer doesn't matter much if you are just trying to be good. My students needed a new vision for prayer: prayer that was radically relational and intimate, prayer that was at home in reality, prayer that was not "fulfilling a quota."[1] But where could they turn for such a vision? Who could be their guide out of the wasteland into the promised land of prayer? This time the Sunday school answer to every question was true: *Jesus.*

Practice the Music

Jesus is not simply *a* human being—Jesus is *the* human being. Jesus is the perfection of the humanity that we only experience as broken. As *the* human being, Jesus is *the* pray-er. When we observe Jesus' life in the Gospels, we discover that prayer was anything but obligatory for him. It was not merely a religious or cultural duty to be performed. He did not pray to be noticed by others. In fact, he had strong words for those who did (Matt. 6:5–6). Rather, prayer was the very essence of what it meant to live in abiding relationship with the Father.

Prayer was personal and intimate.

Prayer was a place for reality.

The tyranny of rote, ritualistic, and de-personalized prayer that shaped my former youth group is crushed under the weight of Jesus' vision of prayer. For Jesus, to pray was to live; to pray was to be human. Prayer was pervasively attached to every aspect of human life. Prayer was a place for raw, uncut, and real engagement with the Father.

The Gospels make it quite clear that Jesus lived in constant abiding relationship with the Father. Jesus was an unceasing pray-er. However, we also find focused times of prayer in Jesus' life. Those focused times of prayer were not attempts to generate a relational connectivity with the Father that did not exist, but rather were the fruit of his abiding relationship with the Father (John 17:11). All Jesus' earthly life was lived in communion with God that was grounded in and fueled by his focused times with God, where he rested in the love of his Father. We dive in to Jesus' life of prayer in this chapter to slowly unravel the cord of prayer that is never broken in the life of Christ.

We, like Jesus, are called to be with God at all times and in all places. We are also called to nurture focused times of prayer that can serve as strategic moments of practicing a posture of rest, attentiveness, and availability to the Father. As we practice prayer, we are learning to cultivate a posture that will orient our everyday lives. I (Jamin) will never forget having a conversation with Eugene Peterson about his personal prayer life.[2] Eugene had a time of focused prayer every morning, an activity he called "spiritual calisthenics." Prayer, he said, didn't really happen until he entered in to the normal, mundane, and sometimes eventful moments of "real" life. It wasn't that his morning prayer was less than real prayer, but that these times oriented the rest of his day. He was acclimating his heart to a certain posture of relational availability.

This is true in all life. If a musician hopes to play violin with the freedom, creativity, and beauty required to participate in a professional symphony, she must practice. We see the same thing in Jesus' life. His life was a perfect symphony harmonized with the glory of God that was grounded in an abiding relationship with the Father. His focused times of prayer continued to recollect, orient, and posture him in the truth of his identity as beloved dust. We're going to further explore the contours of Jesus' life of communion with the Father, but we must begin with his practice—his focused times of prayer—and build from there.

> // And rising very early in the morning, while it was still dark, he departed and went out to a desolate place, and there he prayed. (Mark 1:35)
> // Immediately he made his disciples get into the boat and go before him to the other side, to Bethsaida, while he dismissed the crowd. And after he had taken leave of them, he went up on the mountain to pray. (Mark 6:45–46)
> // But he would withdraw to desolate places to pray. (Luke 5:16)

// In these days he went out to the mountain to pray, and all
night he continued in prayer to God. (Luke 6:12)
// Now it happened that as he was praying alone, the
disciples were with him. (Luke 9:18)
// Now about eight days after these sayings he took with
him Peter and John and James and went up on the
mountain to pray. (Luke 9:28)

The Gospels are riddled with other examples of Jesus'
focused prayer life. He prayed for children (Matt. 19:13–15). He
prayed in the midst of preaching (Matt. 11:25–27). He prayed
for the faith of his friends (Luke 22:31–34). He prayed at meals
(Mark 14:23). He prayed in the face of hardship (Luke 22:39–46).
He prayed upon the cross (Luke 23:34). Jesus prayed, and he
prayed without ceasing. For Jesus, prayer was not merely a duty
or ritual—something you do out of obligation—it was a way of
life. It did not bubble to the surface in certain moments or experiences, but was attached to everything he did. Rather than seeing
his time of focused prayer as one *kind* of activity, and his preaching, healing, and discipling ministry as another *kind* of activity,
they were both connected in his communion with the Father. He
lived out of that communion. Both activities were in place to fuel
and feed his life with God. By communing with God, he lived
according to God's mission in the world. God's mission has a purpose (so he taught, healed, and discipled), and it is grounded in
relationship (so he set aside focused time in prayer so that all life
could be lived in the presence of his Father).

The importance of prayer comes through clearly in Jesus'
teaching on the subject. Jesus taught his disciples how to pray

(Matt. 6:7–15). He taught them to pray in private, rather than be noticed (vv. 5–6). He taught them to ask God for what they desired (Matt. 7:7–12). Jesus taught that exorcism was a prayer-driven ministry (Matt. 17:19–21). The central thrust of Jesus' indictment when he cleared the temple was that it had ceased to be a house of prayer (Mark 11:17). Jesus instructed his disciples to pray for those who persecuted them (Luke 6:28). He taught them to pray with persistence (Luke 18:1–8).

The symphony of Jesus' life was perfect and beautiful but often rhythmically surprising and unexpected. Immediately following his baptism, Jesus was ushered by the Spirit into the wilderness for temptation. At every turn Jesus was confronted and interrupted. Yet the symphony played on to perfection. What anchored Jesus amid the demands of the crowds and the pressure of his ministry was prayer. Jesus turned to the Father in all the ups and downs and twists and turns of his life and ministry. Musical symphonies often take sharp turns in rhythm, and often the hearers encounter surprising shifts and transitions in the notes being played. But there is one thing that remains constant and maintains stability: the pedal tone. The pedal tone is a note played unceasingly throughout the twists and turns taken by the other instruments. The pedal tone in Jesus' life was prayer. The constant theme of prayer on display in the Gospels reveals that prayer was not an occasional act in Jesus' life, but was a defining way of life. It was prayer that served as a stabilizing and constant note throughout his earthly life and ministry.

Praying is a sign of what it means to be beloved. Jesus prayed because he was God's Son. Prayer was a mark of Jesus' abiding life. Rather than being another thing Jesus "did right," prayer was an indication of the posture of his heart. Jesus' rhythm of prayer was not a ritual, but was an intimate and personal dialogue with his Father. Jesus did not have to remember to pray, because prayer was simply *living*. Communion with the Father was not relegated to an occasional check-in, but was an unending embrace of intimacy. *Prayer was being with the Father who was always with him* (John 16:32).

The Sheet Music of Prayer

By now the pedal tone of prayer that grounded Jesus' life should be ringing in our ears. As the masterpiece plays out, one element is easily overlooked: the sheet music that guides it. The sheet music of Jesus' prayer life was the Psalms, the book of Scripture that radically expands our vision of prayer. Studying the Psalms provides a deeper look into the contours and rhythm of Jesus' prayer life. Here, we see the personal depths of prayer; we see that prayer is a place to know God and be known by him.

Jesus' life was shaped by the Psalms. When we see Jesus praying in Gethsemane, we catch glimpses of this connection. Jesus echoed the words of Psalm 42, "My soul is very sorrowful, even to death" (Mark 14:34). Jesus' words at the Last Supper with the disciples directly referenced Psalm 41:9 (John 13:18). Clearly Jesus had absorbed the prayers of the Psalms into his heart. They oriented him to a life lived before the face of God. Graeme Goldsworthy told us Jesus "is recorded as using the Psalms more than any other Old Testament book."[3] Jesus took the words as his own because they spoke the heart of God's people.

Jesus turned to the Psalms as the vocabulary for his prayers. Jesus' prayer life was grounded in the Psalms, which should not surprise us because the Psalms are "the prayerbook of the bible."[4] In Jesus' most agonizing moment on the cross, he quoted the Psalms. First, Jesus said, "My God, my God, why have you forsaken me?" (Mark 15:34; Ps. 22:1). Second, Jesus cried out, "Father, into your hands I commit my spirit!" (Luke 23:46; Ps. 31:5). If we dig a bit deeper, we find that a vast majority of what Jesus said in his final moments of life were references to the Psalms. For instance, on the cross Jesus said, "I thirst" (John 19:28; Ps. 69:21), and "It is finished" (John 19:30; Ps. 22:31).

As a Jew, Jesus grew up with Psalms on his lips. The prayer book of the Psalms had shaped the Jewish people's conversations with God for hundreds of years. He fulfilled every prophecy pointing to the Messiah found within the pages of the Psalms. He gathered all Israel's prayers into himself, and as a result he invited the whole world to pray them *in him*. Jesus said, "These are my words that I spoke to you while I was still with you, that everything written about me in the Law of Moses and the Prophets and *the Psalms* must be fulfilled" (Luke 24:44, emphasis added).[5] As we find our own pain, struggle, and praise through the Psalms, we should find ourselves caught up into the life of God in Christ. He took the plight of humanity into himself, and therefore in him we find the answers to our cries.

As we peruse the pages of Jesus' sheet music, we come to grasp the shape of true prayer. Prayer is situated in the realities of everyday life. It is not a transcendent escape from the tumult of our human relationships, the tedium of labor, the tyranny of our sin, or the temptations of our hearts. The Psalms bring us back down to the dust, remind us of our dustiness, and proclaim that we are beloved all at the same time. The Psalms refuse to accept our habit of separating everyday life from spiritual life that is so endemic in Christian culture today. The Psalms cast a vision for prayer that is focused on the reality of our hearts as a place for relational honesty. It is not a place for pretense, but a place for presentation. *True prayer is a place to know God in the truth of ourselves.* As such it is a place for raw and unbridled emotion. The Psalms themselves run the entire gamut of human affections. John Calvin called the Psalms "an anatomy of all the parts of the soul."[6] That's the vision of prayer that Jesus embraced in an intimate moment before his death.

From Garden to Garden

Prayer is a place of profound relational connection. Jesus' use of the Psalms in his prayer life unveiled this amazing vision of prayer. For many of us, this aspect of Jesus' life remains in the shadows, so here we expose it to the light of day. We need to gaze into Jesus' prayer life with focus and intensity. We need to come into contact with his posture in prayer. We need a scene to truly grasp the texture and quality of his prayer life.

At the beginning of this book, we looked at the garden of Eden. There we learned that we are dust—temporal and finite. We also discovered we are beloved by God. And in the garden, we witnessed humanity's decision to reject those identity markers and embrace the way of dustiness. We watched as Adam and Eve rejected the proper posture of beloved dust and chose to hide and cover. Now, with Christ, we enter a garden once again, the Garden of Gethsemane (Mark 14:32–42). In Eden our eyes were fixed upon Adam; in Gethsemane they will be fixed upon Jesus, the new Adam. In contrast to Adam and Eve's chosen posture in the garden of Eden, in the Garden of Gethsemane Jesus embraced the posture of beloved dust and honesty. What went wrong in the first garden will go right in the second. What was lost will be found. As 1 Corinthians 15:22 states, "For as in Adam all die, so also in Christ shall all be made alive."

Several years ago I (Jamin) decided to take a solitude retreat at a retreat center in Kentucky. The crisp air and dead foliage of the wintery terrain did not deter me from taking an early morning walk. As I embarked to nowhere in particular, a small, disheveled sign caught my eye: "To the statues." I followed the signs, which led through a forest of skeletal trees and around a small pond, until I came upon an open clearing. As I stepped into the hollowed space, the sound of the wind seemed to hush, and I saw two ominous and beautiful statues. One was of the sleeping disciples, and one was of Jesus. It was as though I stepped into a moment of Christ's anguish as a time-traveling bystander. My heart raced as my eyes fixed upon Jesus: on his knees, hands covering his face, crying out to God in prayer. Unbeknownst to the sleeping disciples, it was a moment of earth-shattering proportion and heart-stopping emotion.

The scene in Mark 14:32–42 can leave us startled and perhaps a bit confused. Maybe we enter in to the biblical narrative with the same trepidation I had as I approached the statues in the woods. We come upon the story of Jesus praying in the garden, and we feel like an accidental bystander to something very intimate, very personal, and very important. In this hour of great significance in Jesus' earthly ministry, we are offered a vision of life as beloved dust. We are offered a vision of true prayer. Just as Jesus' knees dug into the soil, we come to see that the way of beloved dust begins in prayer.

In the garden Jesus embraced the posture of dust. He prayed as one who was temporal and finite. Following his historic meal with the twelve, Jesus retreated to a familiar place of prayer.[7] The hour of betrayal was approaching, and Jesus knew it.

> And he took with him Peter and James and John, and began
> to be greatly distressed and troubled. And he said to them,
> "My soul is very sorrowful, even to death. Remain here and
> watch." And going a little farther, he fell on the ground and
> prayed that, if it were possible, the hour might pass from
> him. (Mark 14:33–35)

Immediately we encounter raw and powerful emotion. Jesus was "greatly distressed and troubled." Indeed, Jesus told his disciples that his soul was "very sorrowful."[8] Jesus was overcome with the weight of what was to come. The weight of the decision Adam and Eve made in the first garden was felt in the second garden. It was experienced on the cross. Jesus knew that he would experience relational estrangement from the Father (Mark 15:34). The beloved Son would have to hang on the cross in a posture of shame and guilt as he took on the sins of the world. He not only faced physical death, but spiritual death as well.

The emotionally exposed Jesus can leave us a bit uncomfortable. It is difficult to grasp that this kind of turmoil and distress is known in true peace, true faith, or true courage. Yet, Jesus offered a picture of what it means to be human, and a picture of one who embraces the reality that he is dust. He offered us a picture of what it means to pray as dust. If the emotion is not enough, we see his embrace of finitude and temporality in other elements of the story. We see his finitude as he collapsed upon the ground. On his knees, he was literally postured in humility upon the dust. We see his temporality in his request for the Father to allow the hour of betrayal to pass. As dust he could not overcome the pressing constraints of time and the very real challenges he was about to face.

Rather than rebelling against his limitations, Jesus fully embraced them. Rather than planning an escape route, he prayed. Rather than coordinating his disciples to fight (Peter would have been game), he was on his knees. Surely, the tempting offer Satan had extended him in the wilderness was still on the table: take matters into your own hands, embrace the way of worldly power, for that is the way of glory (Matt. 4:1–11). Unlike Adam and Eve, Jesus did not reject his status as dust. No, the new Adam cast a vision of a *truly* human life.

A life lived as humble dust.

A life marked by honesty before God rather than hiding and covering.

A life grounded in prayer.

Jesus the pray-er not only embraced the posture of dust in the garden, but also the posture of beloved Son. We read in Mark 14:36, "Abba, Father, all things are possible for you. Remove this cup from me. Yet not what I will, but what you will." What is perhaps most vivid about this verse is the relationship within which such a prayer is offered. The address of Jesus' prayer displays the relationship Jesus had with the Father. In his prayer to "Abba" we find Jesus postured as image-bearer, as beloved. The remainder of his prayer shows the dynamics of such a posture. His prayer displays the intimacy, trust, and dependence that are signs of one who knows himself to be beloved.

This vision of Jesus' prayer life feels almost too personal, too intimate. However, we come to this scene as more than accidental bystanders. Much like Peter, James, and John, we are invited to be *with* Jesus. He wants us to see. He wants us to know. Here is prayer. Here is life as beloved dust. Relational. Real. Honest.

The Silence of the Cross

This moment of lonely prayer on a familiar hillside will lead Jesus to another hillside, one unfamiliar and truly solitary. The darkness of Gethsemane is cast by the shadow of the cross to come, the place where the depth of darkness lies. As we mentioned previously, upon the cross Jesus recited the words of the Psalms, "My God, my God, why have you forsaken me?" (Mark 15:34). These words are marked by loneliness, dryness, and emptiness. If we are going to fix our eyes on Jesus the pray-er, we cannot avoid this moment of prayer upon the cross. In his cry from the cross we hear a prayer of honesty much as we did in the Garden of Gethsemane, but perhaps these words grab our hearts with a tighter grip. These are words we have known in prayer or have been fearful to pray ourselves. Perhaps you are experiencing dryness or emptiness in your life. Perhaps as you have read through this book exploring what it means to be with God, you have been asking the questions, "But what if it doesn't feel like God is with me? What if it feels like he has abandoned me or forgotten me?" These are precisely the questions we must take to the cross.

This emotional cry, of course, tells us something of the redemptive reality taking place upon the cross. Despite Jesus' specific work to redeem, there is something of his cry from the cross that we all participate in. Paul told us that we are called to share in the suffering of Christ (Rom. 8:17), and that he rejoices in his sufferings and is "filling up what is lacking in Christ's afflictions for the sake of his body, that is, the church" (Col. 1:24). Jesus himself called us to take up our cross and follow him (Matt. 16:24). The Christian life can rightly be called a cruciform life.[9] We are called to participate in Jesus' suffering, and this includes his suffering in prayer.

As followers of the crucified Lord, we must accept the fact that emptiness or a felt absence of God is going to be part of our journey. This perspective confronts a great deal of what we believe intimate, meaningful relationship should be like. *Surely silence, dryness, or confusion are not markers of a "good" relationship,* we might think. Ponder how people often approach a first date. We have a litmus test for interpreting whether we are making a good connection, communicating well with the person, or have a future with him or her. A moment of awkward dialogue, silence, or simply the absence of exhilaration are enough to deem the date a failure. Emptiness, silence, or confusion are danger signs for us in relationship. Either something is wrong with us, or something is wrong with them. However, this is simply not true.

Real relationship takes place in reality, and reality is that sometimes we will experience disconnection, silence, and confusion. Real relationship is discovered in being with another within these experiences. We struggle with this notion because we have already adopted false presuppositions about how relationships should feel. We think that if we are not carried along by the euphoria of romantic love, then something is broken. This belief, specifically about our relationship with God, is a kind of "prosperity gospel." Prosperity gospels are not simply about receiving money (if you have faith then you will be wealthy), but can be prosperity gospels of excitement, experience, and "meaningful communication." We expect God to give us the feeling we want in prayer, and if he doesn't, we go searching for a way to resolve the problem. We demand an experience, and when God doesn't play by our rules, we either blame him, question his presence, or we turn inward for ways to atone for our own sin (and therefore "buy back" excitement from God).

Think back to a season of your walk with God when nothing seemed to go well. The excitement you once had simply wasn't there. The songs that used to instill a deep sense of the goodness, greatness, and majesty of God droned on as your mind wandered. Instead of longing to read God's Word, maybe the thought of reading it brought up feelings of guilt, pain, or just a sense of being overwhelmed. How you respond to these seasons will tell you a lot about what you believe. Actually, many have argued that the purpose of these seasons is to allow the truth of your beliefs and longings to come to the surface. Why are you so desperate for excitement? Why have you become more concerned with feeling something than about the truth God has proclaimed to you? God often leads his people into the desert to test them and know what is in their hearts (Deut. 8:2). Why should this desert be any different?

God has called his people to holiness and love, but those things are deeply marred by the idolatry that still reigns in the hearts of many Christians. Note how you respond to life when it doesn't go the way you want. Note what you do when God doesn't give you the experience or life you think you deserve. Maybe you turn to some sin you think you need to work on in order to earn what you want. It was in your sin that Christ died for you—why now do you think he rejects you? Furthermore, without Christ you can do nothing (John 15:5), but why now do you think that you can fix the sin in your life to lure him back to you? We can easily play the role of Job's friends to our own consciences, forgetting that Christ has died for such things. Maybe you try to appease God in some way, as if God is a pagan deity that simply wants you to do some things for him and will reward you with excitement, money, etc. Maybe you turn to self-help, thinking you need to learn how to pray the "right way." More often than not, this is an attempt to exercise control over God. If I can figure out the right technique, I can force God's hand.

All these responses, and the many others that may accompany them, are simply idolatry—we have created a false god in our own minds to worship. How we handle our disappointment with God reveals the heart of our idolatry. But that is the very point! The dryness God ushers in to our lives is for the very purpose of bringing these idolatries to the surface. This is why dryness is not a problem to be fixed. This is not a season to work through. This is the high calling of God to be present with him wherever he leads, and to utilize this season to be with him who is always with us, even when we feel like he has abandoned us. If Christ has called us to a cruciform life, we will find ourselves crying out the very same words from the lament Psalms that he did. We will indeed encounter moments of disconnect in prayer. But what do we do with these seasons?

The answer to this challenge is the same we have offered throughout this entire book: be with the God who is always with you. In short, the answer to desolation (dryness) in prayer is *prayer*. As Jesus experienced moments of disconnect and emptiness, he cried out the truth of his heart. So, cry out. If you cannot find your own words, then turn to the sheet music Jesus utilized. The Psalms provide prayerful language untethered to pleasantries. They cut through the facade and give us freedom to yell and cry out, sometimes offensively and irrationally. It is this unbridled poetry that is sanctified text for our experiences with God.

God leads his people into the desert to teach them about himself and to teach them faithfulness. This is a theme in Scripture and was a part of Jesus' own life and ministry. While we cannot go into all the ways God calls us into the dryness of the desert, it is helpful to address some of the spiritual dynamics of these seasons. First, we need to grasp that God is always with us whether we feel his presence or not. God's presence is not tied to our feelings. However, that still doesn't solve the empty feeling we sometimes have when we lean into prayer. The questions that plague us in these seasons often come from a misunderstanding of true relationship, and therefore these times in our lives are used by God to reteach us the nature of real abiding. Mature, deep, and true love does not depend on felt experience. In fact it is precisely these experiences that often form the deepest and most profound caverns of love in our hearts.

I (Jamin) remember spending time with a dear mentor of mine a few years ago. His wife was beginning to experience the dynamics of dementia. Her memory was going, and with it her ability to communicate. I asked him what that was like, and I was shocked by his answer. He opened my eyes to a depth of love I have yet to learn. He told me that there were difficulties, but that this time of their relationship was the best time in all their marriage. "Why?" I asked, somewhat incredulously. "Because, it is based on relationship, not on function. It is not based on an experience she gives me, a depth of conversation that arouses me mentally, but rather on the simple bond of relational, covenantal commitment that unites us." That is love. Love calls us to move into relationship and truly be with the other, regardless of the experience.

Second, God is aware of our lust for experience, our insatiable desire to feel like we are "going somewhere" with this relationship. God is aware of all our idols, even those we are completely unaware of. God has always been aware of them, and therefore isn't simply responding to a recent act of sin, as if you have been especially bad lately and God is leaving. Rather, for whatever reason, God believes you are ready to experience the truth of yourself that, in his patience, he has not exposed you to before. Therefore, in an odd way, these seasons of dryness are one of the greatest gifts God gives us in life. He refuses to reject us, and he also refuses to let us remain saturated in our own brokenness, but he does so patiently. In these seasons we must examine in what ways we turn to self-help, self-atonement, and strategies to find excitement, happiness, or satisfaction, and use these truths of ourselves as opportunities to cast ourselves on the grace of God. These are the idols we are called to throw down and destroy, but we cannot do so on our own. We cannot fix these things, because they are deep movements of our hearts. They are the undercurrents that guide us, but are so deep in our hearts that they are often beneath our consciousness. Instead, we come before God with open hands, holding these things before him. We come before God as idolaters, even as we come before him with the words "nothing but the blood of Jesus" on our lips. As we lean in to the truth of ourselves, in all of our idolatry and brokenness, there will always be new avenues of being with God who is always with us. God is with the true you, and he is calling the true you to come out of hiding to be with him too.

And so, as we experience moments when we cry out, "Why have you forsaken me?" we should not turn to escape, but to resting in Christ. These are not moments to question God's presence, but to trust in it. As we experience these moments in prayer, we are participating in Jesus' life of prayer. We are called into Jesus' own experience of rejection; we do not allow this rejection to define us, but in faith trust that he is with us, calling us into the dark that one day will be light. As we partake in Jesus' cries to his Father, we should also come to partake in his patience.

Jesus, in patience, endured the cross by setting his heart on the joy before him (Heb. 12:2). Likewise, James called Christians to be patient like a farmer (James 5:7–8). The image of a farmer is helpful here. Of the many seasons of crop, only one is the joy of the harvest. The growth of food is a slow process that meanders through several seasons. Likewise, the growth of fruit in the life of a Christian is a slow process that has several seasons. Not all of them are harvest. Our calling is to know patience in seasons that seem purposeless. They are not. These seasons prepare you for the day you will be with God in the fullness of his presence. Until then, our calling is to be with him in the fullness of our brokenness, open to him in the truth of who we are and who he is.

Our Most True Selves

In our own lives, prayer is often confusing and ill-defined. It is distorted and neglected. It is a burden and an obligation. It is reduced to another habit of being a "good" Christian. Prayer is another thing to "work on" or "keep up" in our spiritual life. It is a method in the quest for a more fulfilling, happier life. In all of this the primary question remains: what is prayer? We fail to see that our definitions begin with misguided presumptions, and we continue to perpetuate the same superficial view of prayer facing my intimidated youth group students.

Therefore, the answer to our primary question, "What is prayer?" we have to turn to Jesus. Jesus is *the pray-er*. The symphony of his life was guided by an unceasing prayerful note. He did not pray out of duty. He did not pray under the duress of guilt and shame. He did not pray to get God in line with his plan. Rather, he prayed because he is the Son of the Father. Jesus grasped his identity and as a result cast a vision for life as God intended—a prayerful life. He prayed as beloved dust.

What becomes clear as we observe Jesus praying is that to pray as beloved dust means to pray in reality. We pray in the reality of who we are. We pray as beloved children of the Father. We pray as dusty ones, sinful and broken. We are called to pray in the truth of our identity. If we do not pray in the truth of who we are, then we cannot truly call prayer *being with God*. Being with God implies that we have actually shown up; we are actually present. Prayer is not a place to hide and cover like Adam and Eve in the garden of Eden. It is a place to be honest like Jesus in the Garden of Gethsemane. It is not a place to avoid the truth. In fact, prayer is a place to learn the truth. As Eugene Peterson said, "We are most our true selves when we pray."[10]

And yet, we all are tempted to embrace a false posture in prayer. Perhaps this false posture is sitting in our dustiness. Rather than relating to God from our acceptance in Christ, we try to self-generate righteousness to make him love us. Maybe we don't avoid our sin in prayer, but we sulk in it. We spend our time in prayer brooding, beating ourselves up, and try-ing to manage our dustiness. In effect, prayer becomes a place to commune with ourselves rather than with God. We search within for answers to the problems we uncover and continue to roll around in the dust over and over, thinking it will clean us off just like Dusty the chinchilla. Prayer becomes a place for self-talk, self-fixing, self-condemnation, and self-obsession.

For many of us, it is difficult to receive fully the good news that we are God's beloved. It is hard for us to turn to another for rescue, healing, and redemption. If our earthly parents did not embrace us with unwavering and intimate love, it is challenging to receive our identity as beloved of our heavenly Father. Yet, God is calling us to pray with Jesus, "Abba! Father!" (Rom. 8:15). In contrast, perhaps we embrace the promises of a beloved child while rejecting our status as dust. This may take the form of presuming upon God. Perhaps we treat God like another of life's resources rather than the sovereign Creator of the universe who is beyond our grasp. In effect, we domesticate God to fit our world. Many of us refuse to acknowledge our finitude and temporality in prayer. We stubbornly pretend as if we have things under control in prayer, rather than acknowledging the truth that we are feeble and needy creatures. Yet, God is calling us to pray like Jesus, on our knees in desperate need of the One who is above all things.

If we are honest, prayer feels like a challenge. We have made prayer a chore as opposed to a gracious gift. We have made it a place to project a false self, rather than rest in our true selves. Jesus offered us a different vision of prayer. What we see in Jesus is one who prayed in truth. Jesus prayed from his identity as beloved dust. This is prayer. Not a duty. Not a ritual. Not another "to do." Rather, it is a place of abiding. Prayer is being with God who is always with you. This call to be with God can be a big step; the false postures we have spent years perfecting will not simply be undone by awareness and willpower. These false postures are habits of the heart connected to deep beliefs about God and ourselves that can only be transformed by the work of the Holy Spirit. Our false postures in prayer can only find transformation in prayer itself.

If we give ourselves to the Holy Spirit's work of purging false postures and beliefs, we should take a cue from Jesus. He showed us what it looks like to pray in reality, in the truth of our identity. He pointed us to a resource to put off these false postures in prayer. We have his sheet music. There are 150 prayers in the book of Psalms. We can pray them with Jesus. They can help to locate us in God's redemptive work within. There are psalms of lament, praise, thanksgiving, and confession. As we enter in to the ancient prayers of the people of Israel, God will begin to open up vistas into the truth of our identity in relationship to him. As we pray the words of the Psalms, we will hear the voice of God singing the truth of who we are in light of who he is.

// When I look at your heavens, the work of your fingers, the moon and the stars, which you have set in place, what is man that you are mindful of him, and the son of man that you care for him? (Ps. 8:3–4)

// How long, O LORD? Will you forget me forever? How long will you hide your face from me? How long must I take counsel in my soul and have sorrow in my heart all the day? How long shall my enemy be exalted over me? (Ps. 13:1–2)

// There is no soundness in my flesh because of your indignation; there is no health in my bones because of my sin. For my iniquities have gone over my head; like a heavy burden, they are too heavy for me. (Ps. 38:3–4)

// My flesh and my heart may fail, but God is the strength
of my heart and my portion forever. (Ps. 73:26)

// For you formed my inward parts; you knitted me
together in my mother's womb. I praise you, for I am
fearfully and wonderfully made. (Ps. 139:13–14)

We must not forget that the prayers of the Psalms are God's
Word. As such they are "right" speech. They reveal the truth
of who God is and who we are. They are not simply prayers
offered by men, but are God's revelation. Could there be a better place for us to learn how to pray? As Dietrich Bonhoeffer
insightfully stated about the Psalms,

> The child learns to speak because the parent speaks to the
> child. The child learns the language of the parent. So we
> learn to speak to God because God has spoken and speaks to
> us. In the language of the Father in heaven God's children
> learn to speak with God. Repeating God's own words, we
> begin to pray to God.[11]

Like a child, as we pray the Psalms, we are learning to talk.
We are learning to speak to God. We are learning to relate to
him. We are learning that he is God and we are not. We are
learning that we desperately need his forgiveness. We are learning that by his abounding love and grace our Father calls us his
beloved.

As we pray the prayers of the Psalms, the full picture of our
reality will come into focus. We will be set free to be honest

about our reality and our relationship with God. As we express our true feelings, the seal of pretense is broken, and the cave of the soul is revealed. We put voice to deep feelings of regret, hurt, and pain. We ask him to search us and know us (Ps. 139:23). The poetic words of the Psalms are rhythmic tools of the Holy Spirit to welcome us into reality and invite us to sing with Jesus.[12] In short, the Psalms invite us to pray as Jesus prayed, that our lives may declare, "My heart is steadfast, O God! I will sing and make melody with all my being!" (Ps. 108:1).

SEVEN

FOLLOWING THE ONE
WHO PRAYED //

OUR HEROES ALL have one thing in common. Whether a superhero from a movie or an athlete from our favorite team, one thing remains the same: they all have incredible willpower. Whether it is the determination to stop the bad guy at all costs or the resolve never to quit even when his or her team is losing, a hero in our culture is a person who can dig deep *within him or herself* to find the strength to push through. Quite often we look at Jesus through this cultural lens. We deem him a hero. We think about his life in heroic terms, as if he had just enough intestinal fortitude to make it. As we read about his temptation in the wilderness, his challenges from the Pharisees, and most significantly, his willingness to go to the cross, we think we see a hero with an extraordinary amount of willpower. But is this accurate?

Willpower was *not* the source of Jesus' life of faithfulness; he did not simply dig down deep and force himself through pain, rejection, and trial. He is a hero, no doubt. In fact he is *the* hero. However, it was not intestinal fortitude that enabled Jesus to live the perfect life, but an abiding relationship with the Father by the Holy Spirit (John 14:10). Jesus overcame Satan's temptation, dealt wisely with the Pharisees, and hung on the cross willingly because of this abiding relationship. Jesus rested in the truth of his identity as beloved dust in the hands of his Father. Jesus knew who he was and what he was about because he knew the Father deeply and abided in his love.

Unfortunately we often succumb to the belief that the Christian life is based on self-generated willpower. If we just try a bit harder or come up with the right formula, then perfection will be at our fingertips. As though our personal resolve is all we need to see growth or transformation. This kind of thinking is pervasive in our culture, and it is no more vividly on display than in the American pastime of making a New Year's resolution. Every year as January 1 approaches, gyms, weight-loss groups, and businesses launch major marketing campaigns offering a "better life." This call to make resolutions is once again the temptation of self-help. Advertisements try to convince us that it is possible to self-will our way to happiness. Sadly, in the church, we succumb to the same thing. The tragic irony of this way of approaching growth is that you may resolve to pray more this year, give more this year, or any number of other resolutions, and at no point reference God. You can make a list of things that need to be done and come up with an airtight strategy, but God is irrelevant to the whole process. This is a problem. In Jesus' call to follow him, we find more than just simple imitation; we find something much deeper: abiding.

The Abiding Life

Jesus has surely called us to something deeper than self-help and personal resolve. He has called us to more than trying our best to mimic his behavior. He has called us to abide in him. This begs the question: what does it mean to abide?

Consider these words of Jesus in an intimate moment with his friends:

> I am the true vine, and my Father is the vinedresser. Every branch in me that does not bear fruit he takes away, and every branch that does bear fruit he prunes, that it may bear more fruit. Already you are clean because of the word that I have spoken to you. Abide in me, and I in you. As the branch cannot bear fruit by itself, unless it abides in the vine, neither can you, unless you abide in me. I am the vine; you are the branches. Whoever abides in me and I in him, he it is that bears much fruit, for apart from me you can do nothing. If anyone does not abide in me he is thrown away like a branch and withers; and the branches are gathered, thrown into the fire, and burned. If you abide in me, and my words abide in you, ask whatever you wish, and it will be done for you. By this my Father is glorified, that you bear much fruit and so prove to be my disciples. As the Father has loved me, so have I loved you. Abide in my love. If you keep my commandments, you will abide in my love, just as I have kept my Father's commandments and abide in his love. These things I have spoken to you, that my joy may be in you, and that your joy may be full. (John 15:1–11)

After sharing a meal and washing his disciples' feet, Jesus decided to teach what it meant to follow him, claiming, "I am the true vine." If Jesus was the vine, then what were his disciples? The disciples were the branches extending from the vine. Notice how deep the connection ran between Jesus and his followers. As the vine, Jesus was committed to abiding in the branches. He would remain with them. In turn, the disciples were called to abide in him. They were called to be with the One who was committed to always be with them (Matt. 28:20). They were called to live in union with Christ; to live in dependent relationship with the One who is life (John 14:6). If they wished to produce fruit, they had to abide in him. In contrast, a failure to abide in him would mean a failure to bear fruit. The contrast is made clear when Jesus stated, "Whoever abides in me and I in him, he it is that bears much fruit, for apart from me you can do nothing" (John 15:5). If we abide in him, we will bear *much* fruit. We will flourish. Our lives will be marked by the qualities of love that can only be found in true disciples (Gal. 5:22–23). On the other side of the equation, if we embrace the autonomous way of Adam instead of the way of Jesus, we will be fruitless. When John wrote, "apart from me you can do nothing," he used a double negative in Greek, emphasizing the result of nothingness. In effect, Jesus was saying, "You can do nothing, really nothing!"

If we are not careful, we can read through this entire passage and miss the Father. As the vinedresser, he plays a significant role in this equation of abiding. He determines the fruitfulness of the branches and decides when pruning is necessary. The Father prunes because these are *his* branches and *his* vine. Likewise, the Father appears again as Jesus finished his teaching on abiding, "As the *Father* has *loved me*, so have I *loved you*. Abide in *my love*. If you keep my commandments, you will abide in *my love*, just as I have kept my *Father's* commandments and abide in *his love*" (John 15:9–10, emphasis added). What gives shape and definition to our abiding relationship with Jesus? Jesus' abiding relationship with the Father. Once again the Father-Son relationship establishes the contours of our relationship to God. Jesus offered a picture of this reality throughout the gospel of John.

// So Jesus said to them, "Truly, truly, I say to you, the Son can do *nothing* of his own accord, but only what he sees the Father doing. For whatever the Father does, that the Son does likewise. For the Father loves the Son and shows him all that he himself is doing." (5:19–20a, emphasis added)

// I can do *nothing* on my own. As I hear, I judge, and my judgment is just, because I seek not my own will but the will of him who sent me. (5:30, emphasis added)

// Do you not believe that I am in the Father and the Father is in me? The words that I say to you I do not speak on my own authority, but the Father who dwells in me does his works. (14:10)

// I do not ask for these only, but also for those who will believe in me through their word, that they may all be one, just as you, Father, are in me, and I in you, that they also may be in us, so that the world may believe that you have sent me. (17:20–21)

In Christ we share in the relationship he has with the Father. What is the quality of this relationship? Love. Love is the binding reality of his relationship with the Father, and therefore love binds us to Jesus. Just as Jesus depended on the Father, so, too, are we to depend on Jesus. Just as Jesus did not produce fruit in his life from the strength of his own resolve, but in and through love, so we are called to follow suit. Trying to make life happen in our own strength is the way of Adam, not the way of Christ. It is the way of dustiness.

Praying to the Father

As a pastor, I (Jamin) am constantly asked about prayer. One of the questions that seems to come up rather frequently is: how should I address God in prayer? In other words, when I talk to God in prayer, should I pray to Jesus, do I pray to the Father, or am I praying to the Holy Spirit? Up front, I don't think God is as concerned about our formulas, styles, or grammar in prayer as he is about our hearts (Matt. 6:7–8). That being said, I do believe that Jesus answered this question. He invited us to pray to the Father who loves us. As we pray to the Father, we are praying the prayer of Jesus:

> Pray then like this: "Our Father in heaven, hallowed be your name. Your kingdom come, your will be done, on earth as it is in heaven. Give us this day our daily bread, and forgive us our debts, as we also have forgiven our debtors. And lead us not into temptation, but deliver us from evil." (Matt. 6:9–13)

In a moment of Jesus' personal prayer, the disciples asked him to teach them how to pray, so Jesus gave them an answer. Notice his instruction for prayer began with the words, "Our Father."[1] With those two simple words, Jesus destroyed all forms of moralism and self-engineered spirituality. His was not merely another command for "right behavior" or a model of prayer to mimic. Jesus was not answering a math question, but a profoundly personal and relational question. As N. T. Wright said, "The Lord's Prayer is not so much a command as an invitation: an invitation to share in the prayer-life of Jesus himself."[2] With those two words, Jesus invited us to *pray with him.*

He invited us to pray as the beloved of the Father.

He invited us to participate in his prayer—the prayer of the Son to the Father (Luke 10:21).

When Jesus called God "my Father," we are told the Jews wanted to kill him (John 5:17–18). Calling God "my Father" was claiming equality with God. This is the bold proclamation of the Christian gospel. In Christ we pray "our Father" with the one who prays "my Father." The only one who could pray "*my* Father" was the true Son. The "our" is not simply to remind us that we pray with the community of the saints, which we do. Rather, we pray *our* Father because we pray with Jesus. Jesus called us into his prayer-life with the Father, and so we, too, pray, "Father."

All prayer is personal and relational. Eugene Peterson reminded us, "The minute we obliterate the personal from prayer, there is no prayer. The heart stops beating."[3] How Jesus addressed God in prayer should not appear new to us—it is how

Jesus addressed God all along. In the Garden of Gethsemane, Jesus called God "Abba." In the immediate context of Jesus' teaching on the Lord's Prayer in the Sermon on the Mount, Jesus used the term *Father* fifteen times.[4] It is that invitation to participate in his prayer life that the apostle Paul made so clear when he said, "For you did not receive the spirit of slavery to fall back into fear, but you have received the Spirit of adoption as sons, by whom we cry, 'Abba! Father!'" (Rom. 8:15) "And because you are sons, God has sent the Spirit of his Son into our hearts, crying, 'Abba! Father!'" (Gal. 4:6)

Where does this prayer to Abba begin? What sets its course? Prayer does not begin with us, but with the Father. The starting place of prayer is God and his action. We rest in who he is. God governs prayer. He who set the course of the universe sets the course of our prayers. If we are not careful, we can read these initial declarations of who God is as cold affirmations of generic belief statements. Rather, we proclaim who God is and we submit to such truths within the context of an intimate Father-child dialogue. These truths are known and experienced in relationship with the Father. The first lines of the Lord's Prayer are a personal recognition of who we know God to be.

"Our Father in heaven, hallowed be your name."

"Your kingdom come, your will be done, on earth as it is in heaven."

Jesus made it clear that we address a Father who is "in heaven." He is holy. He is above us. As we saw in chapter 3, we cannot ascend to God (Tower of Babel), but rather, he always descends to us. He is set apart. His name is to be "hallowed." We are to give him honor, glory, and praise. His name is above every name, including ours. Again, we are reminded of the people of Babel who foolishly sought to make their name great. That is not the way of Jesus. Of course, this statement also echoes the first three of the Ten Commandments: "You shall have no other gods before me. You shall not make for yourself a carved image, or any likeness of anything that is in heaven above, or that is in the earth beneath, or that is in the water under the earth. You shall not bow down to them or serve them" (Ex. 20:3–5).[5] The same God who gives these commands is the God we are praying to, and as we begin our prayers, we acknowledge who it is we are speaking with. In so doing, we acknowledge something about ourselves.

He is Creator, and we are creature.

He is infinite, and we are finite.

He is eternal, and we are temporal.

He is the king, and so we ask that his "kingdom come" and "his will be done, on earth as it is in heaven." Jesus inaugurated his kingdom on earth, but the kingdom has yet to come in its fullness. To pray "your kingdom come" is at once a celebration of the truth that in Jesus the kingdom of God is indeed "at hand" (Mark 1:15), while at the same time it is a declaration of hope for the consummation of the kingdom to come. When we pray "your kingdom come," we say yes to Jesus' present kingdom initiative, and we long for its ultimate fulfillment. We ask for the *not yet* to arrive—for Christ to come again to reign fully and completely over all things. We seek his reign, his way, and his life as we seek to abide in his presence. Of course, this means we believe God's kingdom initiative is good and right. It is something worth living for. It is something worth dying for. We acknowledge his good, pleasing, and perfect will. So we pray "his will be done, on earth as it is in heaven." We desire his will to be done here with the same immediacy with which it is done in heaven. We recognize that his ways are above our ways, and we ask that his ways become our ways. We seek a heart in harmony with his plan and program. We pursue his end and goal above our own.

This was the prayer God was inviting me into when I (Jamin) lost my job. As I prayed this prayer, I realized I wanted my will, not his. Perhaps more specifically, I wanted my will to be his will. But this prayer invites us to a new kind of posture, a posture of receiving that his ways are above our ways. We ask that he have his way in us and in his world. We ask that he transform and reorder our hearts. As we do, we come to know him as Lord and King.

This first half of Jesus' invitation to pray is not merely a formula for our use, but a way of prayer known *personally* to Jesus. Jesus is inviting us to pray his prayer. He has prayed to the Father who is in heaven: "When Jesus had spoken these words, he lifted up his eyes to heaven" (John 17:1). He has hallowed the Father's name in prayer: "Father, glorify your name" (John 12:28). He prayed that his will be done: "Yet not what I will, but what you will" (Mark 14:36). As we continue in the Lord's Prayer, we encounter three key phrases that turn toward human needs. Having begun with who God is, we acknowledge who we are: we are dust, needy and dependent; we are dusty, sinful, and selfish. However, the truth of who God is does not get left behind. As each request rolls off our tongues, we are acknowledging God is God, and he is with us. Each phrase reminds us that we live our lives—even the most mundane aspects of our lives—*with* him: "Give us this day our daily bread." "Forgive us our debts, as we also have forgiven our debtors." "Lead us not into temptation, but deliver us from evil."

We pray that God, who is above all things, would provide for our most basic needs. We acknowledge we are temporal and finite, and just like the Israelites we need his manna to survive. We are dependent on him for life each day. We also pray that he forgives our debts because we are still marked by the way of dustiness. Rather than lifting our hands toward heaven above, we continue to clutch the earth below. Rather than desiring his will to be done, we desire our will to be done. As those who continue to bathe in the dust, we are to drop to our knees in a posture of repentance. Finally, we ask God to guard us from temptation in times of trial. We ask him to protect us from the evil one. As people living in the already-but-not-yet kingdom, we recognize that "we do not wrestle against flesh and blood, but against the rulers, against the authorities, against the cosmic powers over this present darkness, against the spiritual forces of evil in the heavenly places" (Eph. 6:12). This petition echoes Jesus' exhortation to the disciples in the Garden of Gethsemane when he told them to "watch and pray that you may not enter into temptation" (Mark 14:38). As we pray these words, we remember the other garden this story began in, and we recall Adam and Eve's temptation. With these final words of the Lord's Prayer, we ask for God's protection, deliverance, and mercy.

In these final petitions we are again reminded that Jesus prays with us, and we pray in him. Jesus' temptation in the wilderness gives us a picture of one who knew what it was to need daily bread while at the same time trusting God to provide regardless of circumstances (Matt. 4:1–11). Jesus experienced temptation in his testing as Satan offered him a way out. And Jesus prayed for forgiveness from a unique position. First, he prayed for forgiveness not for himself, but for us: "Father, forgive them, for they know not what they do" (Luke 23:34). Second, as Eugene Peterson reminded us, "He joins us where we are, mired in the mud of sin ('became sin for us': see 2 Cor. 5:21). He takes his place alongside us and invites us to pray with him, 'Forgive us . . .'"[6] Jesus knew the Father as gracious provider and sovereign protector. He experienced these realities of the Father's character in prayer. He knew the Father in whom he abided. Likewise, Jesus' invitation to pray with him to the Father was an invitation to know the Father as provider and protector. As we come to know him as provider and protector—as *our* Father—we rest in his loving embrace.

The Lord's Prayer is a prayer of beloved dust. As such, it is not merely a formula or mantra for prayer, but a profound theology of prayer. In the words of N. T. Wright, "the Lord's Prayer may be seen as being to the church as the Ten Commandments were to Israel: not just something to do, a comparatively arbitrary rule of life, but the heart of the new covenant charter."[7] In this invitation to pray, Jesus grounded our identity as those found in him. He welcomed us to pray to the Father in the truth of who we are. The Lord's Prayer orients us to God's transcendence and sovereignty as well as his presence and care. As we pray this prayer *with* Jesus, we are reminded that God is Creator and we are creature; we are reminded that he calls us to be with him as he is with us.

Praying with the Pray-er

Jesus defined what prayer is for us. As *the* pray-er, he gave us a perfect picture of prayer. He answered the question, "What is prayer?" Prayer is being with God who is always with us. As such, it is a place to know God and be known by God. For those who are called beloved dust, prayer is not merely an act, but a grounding reality of life. To pray is to abide. As John 15 indicates, we are to abide in Jesus who is abiding in us. Jesus is committed to us. He will be with us. This may sound odd to us because we often view Jesus as one who *lived* and not also as the one who *lives*. We are so accustomed to asking, "What would Jesus do?" that we neglect to ask, "What is Jesus doing?" He who was resurrected from the dead continues to live in us by his Holy Spirit.

// I will ask the Father, and he will give you another Helper, to be with you forever, even the Spirit of truth, whom the world cannot receive, because it neither sees him nor knows him. You know him, for he dwells with you and will be in you. I will not leave you as orphans; I will come to you. Yet a little while and the world will see me no more, but you will see me. Because I live, you also will live. In that day you will know that I am in my Father, and you in me, and I in you. (John 14:16–20)

// I have been crucified with Christ. It is no longer I who live, but Christ who lives in me. And the life I now live in the flesh I live by faith in the Son of God, who loved me and gave himself for me. (Gal. 2:20)

Jesus is with us, and we have life in him. Jesus did not merely pray as *a* human, but as *the* human. He set a new course, established the way (John 14:6), and welcomed us in. So Jesus' example, as seen in the previous chapter, is more than a mere reminder to do "the right things," but is an invitation. It is an invitation we can truly call *good news*. This good news is found cloaked in what appears to be bad news: "I tell you the truth: it is to your advantage that I go away, for if I do not go away, the Helper will not come to you. But if I go, I will send him to you" (John 16:7). Jesus' ascension is not a loss, but rather a gain. By the Holy Spirit we can be in union with Christ always. The one who is constantly abiding in relationship with the Father by the Holy Spirit has invited us to do the same. He invites us to participate in his life of prayer. He invites us to be with *our Father* who is always with us in Christ.

Recreated for Prayer

Our lives are found in Jesus. We don't stand in the present looking back at Jesus as a figure in history. We stand with him who wraps us in his life of love here and now. We share in the divine Father-Son relationship. As adopted sons and daughters, we are claimed and bound in the same relationship of intimacy. Our identity is shaped by the truth that in Christ, the Father calls us his own. We are invited yet again to embrace the truth of our finitude and temporality as we receive the truth that apart from him we can do nothing. We are invited to rest in the arms of the one who said "abide in my love."

Jesus Christ is *the* true human being; he became beloved

dust and dwelt among us. As the new Adam, he redeemed what had been lost in the first Adam (Rom. 5:17). Jesus, the Word of God, spoke creation into existence and was fully and truly human in the incarnation. He became beloved dust in order to invite us dusty ones into our true identity in him. He invites those who have participated in the history of Adam to participate in his history. The focal point of this history is the life, death, resurrection, and ascension of Jesus Christ, and now that history is the shape of our lives.

How does this impact prayer? Just as we were *created for prayer*, in Christ we have been *recreated for prayer*. To be a new creation means that in Christ we have been brought near to the Father. As 2 Corinthians 5:21 heralds, "For our sake he made him to be sin who knew no sin, so that in him we might become the righteousness of God." We have been reconciled to right relationship with God, and as such invited to *be with him* yet again, to pray.

Our most fundamental act is prayer because it fuels all our actions as *prayerful* responses to God. We join Jesus in prayer in a way and to a degree that is ultimately a spiritual mystery. We participate in his prayer by the Holy Spirit. We cry out to Abba. In Christ, we can know God and be known by God. As P. T. Forsyth said, "Our prayer is the momentary function of the Eternal Son's communion and intercession with the Eternal Father."[8] Our prayers are caught up in the life and communication of the triune God. In prayer we can truly say that once we were lost, but now we are found (Luke 15:24), and at the same time we find ourselves lost again as we are engulfed by the peace of God which surpasses all understanding (Phil. 4:7).

Grasping Prayer

Knowledge is a loaded word in our culture. When we hear it, we immediately fill it with meaning. Knowledge is typically associated with information or facts. I may *know* a lot about something or someone because of the information I have learned, but this definition of knowledge limits the real scope of the word. This definition is merely knowledge *about,* but neglects knowledge *of.* Knowledge of something or someone involves experience and intimacy. I may know a lot about a particular actor because I read information about him or her online (assuming it is true). I may know where the actor lives, whom he is dating, or what he likes to eat, but this does not mean that I truly know him. I have knowledge *about* him, but I do not have knowledge *of* him. Unless I actually meet the actor, spend time with him, dialogue with him, etc., I don't know him.

Oddly, we can also have very little knowledge *about* someone and yet have a lot of knowledge *of* them. This is true with my (Jamin) children. When my kids were two years old, they could not have told you where I worked, how old I was, where I had gone to seminary, or what my favorite food was. They had very little knowledge *about* me. Yet they had deep, intimate, and meaningful knowledge *of* me. My kids knew their dad because they spent time with me, because they experienced who I was in loving relationship. The experiences of cuddling on the couch, wiping away tears, reading stories, and even disciplining them taught my children who I was. They know who I am. They know I am Dad. They know me because we spend time together and are present with one another.

When we are in relationship, knowledge *of* is much more

important than knowledge *about*. Knowledge *about* someone is merely intended to support our knowledge *of* him or her. With childlike love and innocence, we are called to know God, to abide in relationship with him. Regardless of how many seminary classes we have taken or Bible studies we have attended, we can know him because he is a Father who wants to be known by his children. We know him because he chooses to be known. In prayer we come to know this God of glory, who is sovereign provider, forgiver, and protector. As we come to have knowledge of God as heavenly Father, we in turn know ourselves. This shapes our entire Christian lives. John Calvin said, "true and sound wisdom consists of two parts: the knowledge of God and of ourselves." Calvin went on to add that we only really know ourselves if we have "contemplated the face of God" and then immediately contemplate ourselves.[9]

As we know ourselves as beloved dust, we share with God the everyday realities of our lives. Prayer is a place to be known. We don't pray to give God information he does not know, but to rest in the profound truth that he knows more about it than we do. He knows what we need. He knows our sin. He knows what we face. Our Heavenly Father is well acquainted with his children. Sometimes in prayer we think we need to be clear or profound for God to "get it." We want to make sure he understands. We want to make sure we are not missed. We want to make sure he knows us. As we struggle with words, he is calling us to rest in the truth that he already has profound knowledge of us.

> Likewise the Spirit helps us in our weakness. For we do not
> know what to pray for as we ought, but the Spirit himself
> intercedes for us with groanings too deep for words. And he

who searches hearts knows what is the mind of the Spirit,
because the Spirit intercedes for the saints according to the
will of God. (Rom. 8:26–27)

One afternoon, my (Jamin) four-year-old daughter picked
up her mom's phone and sent me a text message that had about
fifteen letter *g*'s, ten letter *l*'s, and twelve letter *k*'s in it. It was
indistinguishable and garbled. The moment I saw the text, I
knew who it was from, and I knew she wanted to send me a
text but didn't know how. I knew my daughter's voice even
though it came through unclear and incoherent. I smiled as I
read that incoherent text, and I thought, *That's my little girl.*
In the same way, God receives our jumbled communication
and incoherent self-articulation with a smile and a fatherly
embrace. He knows us fully, and even amid what we feel is
unclear and confusing, he is seeing us for who we truly are, his
beloved children. As those who are in Christ, we are always
received by the Father.

In prayer the Father cherishes us.

In prayer the Father calls us his own.

In prayer the Father loves us.

EIGHT

WITH GOD IN THE TEMPLE //

IT WAS A hot summer day in Greece. As we hiked to the top of the Acropolis, the view of Athens was spectacular. We finally arrived at our destination, the Parthenon. This magnificent temple has stood for more than two thousand years. I (Jamin) sat down on the edge of the steps, and the size of the columns and the sheer beauty of the ancient architecture overwhelmed me. My eyes scanned the horizon where I could see other ancient buildings still standing in the distance. I could picture the temple in its heyday, towering over a bustling city. I could imagine Paul's eyes fixed upon this spectacular demonstration of Greek architecture as he entered Athens.

Unfortunately, unlike my experience on the Acropolis, when we come across the temple in Scripture, our minds glaze over. It feels outside the reach of our imaginations. The sacrifices, the money-changers, and the rituals feel so completely foreign and odd that we rarely stop and meditate on its significance. If we do at all, our focus tends to be on the temple's importance in history or its role in the end times. We do not ask why it matters for us now. But the New Testament is saturated with temple imagery and illusions, many of which are so subtle that our eyes pass over these important points without illuminating their value. As we continue to build on all that we have already talked about, we have to address the temple.

The temple was the place where the people of God came to be in God's immediate presence. God was always with them no matter where they were, no doubt, but not in the same way he was present in the temple. Each area of the temple—the outer court, the holy place, and the holy of holies—increased in holiness. The holy of holies was where God's full presence was known on earth—a place so holy that only the high priest could enter once a year (and even then fearing for his life). But Stephen, the first Christian martyr, exposed tension to these truths: "Yet the Most High does not dwell in houses made by hands, as the prophet says, 'Heaven is my throne, and the earth is my footstool. What kind of house will you build for me, says the Lord, or what is the place of my rest? Did not my hand make all these things?'" (Acts 7:48–50). Jesus, furthermore, predicted the destruction of the temple, because God's plan was not simply to localize his presence (Mark 13:2). God's desire was that his presence would permeate all creation.

With Jesus we have a new kind of temple assembled by God. When Jesus ascended, he ascended to the true temple "that the Lord set up, not man" (Heb. 8:2). We do not hope in what our hands have created, but in Christ who walked in our nature in a place we could never go. "For Christ has entered, not into holy places made with hands, which are copies of the true things, but into heaven itself, now to appear in the presence of God on our behalf" (Heb. 9:24). After his death and resurrection, just as in his childhood, Jesus could say, "Why were you looking for me? Did you not know that I must be in my Father's house?" (Luke 2:49). Jesus has ascended to his Father's house in heaven to fulfill his call. Therefore, we must turn our eyes to heaven.

Starting at the End

Kids' placemats at restaurants used to thrill me (Kyle) as a child. After a couple of games of tic-tac-toe and a word search puzzle, I would set my sights on the maze. After two or three half-hearted attempts to navigate the maze correctly, I would intuitively start at the end and work my way to the beginning. It was always much easier. With prayer, we do the same. Jesus' life orients our prayer lives, but we must not diminish the scope of Jesus' whole life. Jesus is still alive. Therefore we are confronted with the question: how does Jesus' life in heaven help us understand prayer? We turn to this question in our last two chapters.

One of the great surprises in Scripture is God's presence breaking in to creation. In chapter 1 we saw his presence in the garden of Eden and the original purpose of creation as the realm of God's presence. Then we saw the temple, which was God's localized presence to his people that was superseded by Jesus. At the end of the biblical narrative, similarly, we find the movement of God's presence reaching perfection. Creation exists to be saturated with God's presence. The goal of creation was "God's presence filling the entire creation in the way it had formerly filled only the holy of holies."[1] The original garden was a type of temple that God left Adam to preside over. That garden-temple was to be cultivated to increase across the earth "so that the earth would be completely filled with God's glorious presence."[2] The temple, therefore, serves as a helpful way to turn our eyes to the end, to the purpose of God's movement in redemption history. This is exactly what we see at the end of Revelation:

> I saw the holy city, new Jerusalem, coming down out of heaven from God, prepared as a bride adorned for her husband. And I heard a loud voice from the throne saying, "Behold, the dwelling place of God is with man. He will dwell with them, and they will be his people, and God himself will be with them as their God. He will wipe away every tear from their eyes, and death shall be no more, neither shall there be mourning, nor crying, nor pain anymore, for the former things have passed away." (21:2–4)

God's purpose in creation finds its fulfillment here, where God's presence descends to his people. God creates a people for himself, and his presence brings healing, peace, and joy, pounding the final nail in the coffin of death. On our journey of faith, this is where we are headed.

The New Jerusalem is clearly not a normal city. John was given a measuring rod to measure the city: "The city lies foursquare, its length the same as its width" (Rev. 21:16). The city was twelve thousand stadia—its length, height, and width all equal. The city was pure gold, like glass (Rev. 21:17–18). Importantly, John told us,

I saw no temple in the city, for its temple is the Lord God the Almighty and the Lamb. And the city has no need of sun or moon to shine on it, for the glory of God gives it light, and its lamp is the Lamb. By its light will the nations walk, and the kings of the earth will bring their glory into it, and its gates will never be shut by day—and there will be no night there. (Rev. 21:22–25)

While incredible and awe-inspiring, the imagery is not necessarily what we would consider clear. It reads like a dream, making sense in the moment but growing increasingly fuzzy over time. It raises questions: Why is the New Jerusalem a huge cube? Why is it covered in gold? It's impressive, but isn't it a bit gaudy? The reason is simple, but far from obvious. This image of the New Jerusalem is depicting the holy of holies from the temple overtaking all creation. John was shown a city that was square, or cubic, because the holy of holies was such a shape (1 Kings 6:20).[3] What John saw was that the place of God's absolute presence to his creation had become creation itself. Furthermore, the New Jerusalem is shown to be paved with gold because the holy of holies was covered in gold. The New Jerusalem has no temple because the heart of the temple—the holy of holies—is the New Jerusalem itself. We are told that the servants of God will worship him, and "they will see his face, and his name will be on their foreheads" (Rev. 22:3–4). Biblical theologian G. K. Beale explained, "Whereas the high priest, who wore God's name on his forehead, was the only person in Israel who could enter the holy of holies once a year and be in God's presence, in the future all of God's people will become high priests with God's 'name on their foreheads' and standing, not one day a year, but forever in God's presence."[4]

This vision of our future is nothing short of staggering. In the image of the temple, we see the big picture of God's plan for his world. God created his world so that he could permeate it with his presence. God breathed life into the dust so that he could commune with the people he raised from the ground. In Christ we see the lengths to which God is willing to go to make this plan happen. What we see in Revelation is the implication of Christ's ascent to the right hand of God. The heavenly temple will one day descend to incorporate all those with faith into the fullness of God's presence and life. We now know this in our own lives, however limited our grasp, because of the presence of the Spirit. Whereas, "the temple's centre of gravity during the church age is located in the heavenly realm . . . it has begun to invade the earthly through the Spirit in the church."[5] In the light of God's perfect presence, humanity functions as it was supposed to. Perfect society happens in the presence of Christ. The church is now the place where this presence begins to shine through the broken cracks of the world.

Taste and See

God creates a perfect human society by giving his presence in abundance. What started as a garden in Genesis is now a city in Revelation. In the image of the New Jerusalem, we are told that God will break open his own life and pour it out to his creation. At the closing of Revelation we are told, "let the one who is thirsty come; let the one who desires take the water of life without price" (22:17). God is the fountain of love who pours himself out in abundance to his people. We are called to be the thirsty ones satisfying ourselves on the grace of God. As told to us by Peter, "Like newborn infants, long for the pure spiritual milk, that by it you may grow up into salvation—if indeed you have tasted that the Lord is good" (1 Peter 2:2–3). We should taste that the Lord is good, knowing the delight of giving ourselves fully to God. In the end, we will overflow with the love and beauty of God poured out to us. Now we know this through a mirror dimly (1 Cor. 13:12). As we set our eyes in hope on this future reality, we rest in the fact that we have been given the down payment of that future in the Spirit (Eph. 1:14).

As we have seen, the main purpose of Christ's work is to break open God's life of love to bring us to the Father. "For Christ also suffered once for sins, the righteous for the unrighteous, that he might bring us to God" (1 Peter 3:18). In redeeming us, Christ has put us on track to be with God. There is a sense, of course, that this is already the case. We already noticed that our lives are "hidden with Christ in God" (Col. 3:3). Furthermore, Paul told us that our old selves were crucified with Christ, so we know that we will be united to him in his resurrection (Rom. 6:5–6). Jesus, God's own Son, has pulled us into himself as sons and daughters of God, justified, adopted, and redeemed before the Father. Our lives are hidden with Christ in God because Christ is our surety. In light of this reality, we are called to draw near to God.

A Better Hope

As those redeemed by Christ to be brought before the Father, we draw near to the Father in Christ. Once again, this leads us to think a bit more about the temple. Jesus is our High Priest who has ascended to the right hand of the Father into the eternal temple made without hands. The priesthood in the Old Testament was a broken sign of Christ's priesthood. As the author of Hebrews explained, "a former commandment is set aside because of its weakness and uselessness (for the law made nothing perfect); but on the other hand, a better hope is introduced, through which we draw near to God" (Heb. 7:18–19). This better hope is Jesus, as our eternal High Priest who has offered a sacrifice for our sins in his own blood:

> He has no need, like those high priests, to offer sacrifices daily, first for his own sins and then for those of the people, since he did this once for all when he offered up himself. For the law appoints men in their weakness as high priests, but the word of the oath, which came later than the law, appoints a Son who has been made perfect forever. (Heb. 7:27–28)

Therefore, "he is able to save to the uttermost those who draw near to God through him, since he always lives to make intercession for them" (Heb. 7:25).

Because Christ took on dust, we can now draw near to the Father. This is a call to pray from the depths of our new reality *in Christ*. As those who have been pulled into the life of God in Christ, we do not pray as aliens or foreigners, but as children of God. We pray as people who can claim the High Priest as one of their own. This High Priest stands before the Father, perfect in both his divinity and humanity. In light of this, the author of Hebrews once again offered us an admonition: "Let us then with confidence draw near to the throne of grace, that we may receive mercy and find grace to help in time of need" (Heb. 4:16). With all our timidity, sin, fear, anxiety, and brokenness, we approach the throne of grace boldly because we approach it as those *in* Christ. We do not pave the way there through our accomplishments—we approach the throne by the blood of Christ. This is not something we simply affirm; this must shape the posture of our hearts in prayer. We come before God humbly, boasting in Christ alone.

Praying in the Temple

To understand this, let's step back for a minute. We have seen the temple move from a tent, to a temple, to Christ, to where the innermost part of the temple (the holy of holies) overtakes reality. This progression in the redemption of God takes strides to perfection.[6] In the future there is no need for a temple because God's presence saturates the city of God. Now, heaven hosts the holy of holies because that is where the presence of God is fully. By the grace of God and the sending of his Spirit, believers exist as priests in the spiritual presence of God. We are all called to mediate his presence to the world, serving and offering ourselves in his service. But we also feel the tension of the age in which we live, an age marked by Christ's redemption and yet by sin's stain and infiltration. In this age, we are called to present our bodies as living sacrifices, holy and acceptable to God, which is our spiritual worship (Rom. 12:1). Our spiritual acts of worship, corresponding to the sacrifices of the old temple, is a part of our drawing near to the God of grace. In the old temple, God's people drew near to him through sacrifices for their sins and uncleanliness. They came in humility (or they should have) by laying down sacrifices to the Lord as an act representing the laying down of their lives.

Let's pause to consider this. One of the great temptations in the sacrificial system is being so overcome by the technique of it all that you forget the purpose of the sacrifice in the first place. People easily make sacrifice mechanistic. You sin, so you have to push the right buttons and pull all the right levers to fix it. By focusing on getting the technique right, you forget there is no direct connection between your action and forgiveness. In other words, there is nothing connecting the killing of an animal with God's forgiveness, as if God was bound to forgive as long as someone knew the correct formula.

God designed all the aspects of the temple, from the priest to the techniques, to point to the heavenly temple. By entering the temple for forgiveness, cleansing, and prayer, you were entering God's presence. The second you took your eyes off of God, you quickly missed the point. What is seen blinds you to the truth of the unseen. We are to "look not to the things that are seen but to the things that are unseen. For the things that are seen are transient, but the things that are unseen are eternal" (2 Cor. 4:18). God calls us to look beyond the technique of seeking forgiveness, to the real purpose—communion with God. This is the great tragedy that continues to stain humanity. We seek to *use* God when he is calling us to commune with him.

Unlike those living under the old sacrificial system, we are in a much different place. Our lives are lived in the shadow of Christ's perfect sacrifice, and so we draw near in the confidence of what he has done. This drawing near is an action of our whole lives—lives lived in the temple of God (God's presence by grace). This, however, does not eliminate the temptation to focus on technique. All too often we take our eyes off of Christ to focus on "getting it right." Like the husband who thinks that flowers can fix any problem and therefore fails to attend to and love his wife truly, we look for ways to cover and hide our brokenness rather than commune with God. But in Christ, that is exactly what we have been offered: communion. In light of this, we can proclaim with the author of Hebrews, "since we have confidence to enter the holy places by the blood of Jesus, by the new and living way that he opened for us through the curtain, that is, through his flesh, and since we have a great priest over the house of God, let us draw near with a true heart in full assurance of faith, with our hearts sprinkled clean from an evil conscience and our bodies washed with pure water" (10:19–22). We have been sprinkled clean by the blood of Christ. Therefore our calling as those of faith is to draw near to God in Christ Jesus. That calling is the way of prayer.

We draw near to God through our great High Priest as we enter the holy place of the heavenly temple. We come here in prayer. In prayer, we stand before the throne of grace as those who are redeemed. We stand as dust. Here we come before God on bended knee, saying, "Remember, my Lord, I am but dust" (Ps. 103:14).

Our Identity at the Throne of Grace

Even as we come before God as dust, we stand there as his beloved. Drawing near to God is drawing near to God in faith, and therefore in Christ. Drawing near to God is trusting that "without faith it is impossible to please him, for whoever would draw near to God must believe that he exists and that he rewards those who seek him" (Heb. 11:6). In faith we draw near to God, and therefore our prayers must be prayers of faith. Praying in faith is not trying hard to believe that prayers are answered when you don't believe they are. Prayers of faith are drawing near to God in Christ Jesus. Those who pray in faith enter God's throne room with confidence, not because of their merits or efforts, but because they enter on the merit and standing of Christ. You do not stand before a holy God unclothed. Just as in the garden God clothed his people in the midst of their sin, you come dressed in Christ's robes of righteousness. You stand before God as beloved dust.

One of the great mistakes in prayer is to think that our prayers ascend to God and are sifted through a "quality prayer filter." We can subconsciously think that God is waiting to hear certain key phrases or tones, or has a specific timetable he uses, as if prayers that are under a minute long just won't make it through the density of the prayer filter. Rather, just as we are justified, redeemed, accepted, and adopted by God, so are our prayers.[7] My prayers are accepted because of Christ. I am allowed to draw near to God because God has drawn near to me in Christ. My life is hidden with Christ in God. Therefore, in our prayers we can draw near in confidence that we are heard, accepted, and received by the Father of mercy.

Jesus told a different story in Matthew 7: "On that day many will say to me, 'Lord, Lord, did we not prophesy in your name, and cast out demons in your name, and do many mighty works in your name?' And then will I declare to them, 'I never knew you; depart from me, you workers of lawlessness'" (vv. 22–23). As these people stood before Christ, they were asked, presumably, "Who are you?" This question, or one like it, was answered with a list of achievements. "Look at the kinds of things I did. Look at the kind of person I was. Look what I did *in your name*." Christ responded that he did not know them. They, of course, did not know him either.

The question, "Who are you?" is somewhat similar to the question God asked Adam and Eve in the garden: "Where are you?" The nature of the question already determines the answer. Christ had to ask, "Who are you?" because those in Matthew 7 claiming allegiance with Jesus were not known. Similarly, God had to ask Adam and Eve, "Where are you?" because they were hiding, and therefore, were proving the effects of sin. Just as Adam and Eve chose to hide and cover, so these people chose achievements to hide and cover from God. Both acts of hiding and covering fail to grasp who God is and who they are. Before the face of God, there is no hiding or covering. In his presence there is only perfect knowledge. The only appropriate response to God's inquiry, "Who are you?" is to proclaim, "I am yours." Pointing to Jesus and claiming, "All I have is Jesus" is the response to our frailty, not proclaiming our impressive ministry résumé.

Far from being an isolated issue for Judgment Day, this is exactly what we do in prayer. When we draw near to God in prayer, we do not, or should not, pepper it with things we have done for him to justify ourselves in his presence. We do not pray from our achievements, accolades, or social standing. We pray from our vulnerability and humility, and ultimately, from our only hope. We do not rest in ourselves, but in another: *Jesus.* We pray as those in Christ, and therefore literally pray "in Jesus' name." We do not come to the Father in our own names, nor do we come to him in what we have achieved in Jesus' name. We come under Christ's achievement. For those who draw near to God in faith, anything else they can say is now finally understood as rubbish (Phil. 3:8). Everything that is ours is thrown down as meaningless next to the insurmountable greatness of what Christ has done for us.

Praying His Name in Vain

"In the name of Jesus." These are the words that tell us when someone is about to finish praying. Or, are they more than that? While we all pray in the name of Jesus, it can be easy to neglect what that really says about our prayers. Praying in this fashion easily becomes another thing we do that we don't think much about. But praying in this way defines and shapes what prayer is.

One of the reasons why we fail to think much about praying in Jesus' name is because we often subconsciously relegate Jesus to earthly history. We look back to him in history as little more than a great teacher, someone whose life we should emulate. He becomes little more than an example of good behavior. We, of course, want to claim that his life (particularly his death) was important, but now we must work hard to imitate his life. We come to believe that we must become good people, if for no other reason than out of gratitude for what he has done.

Life in Christ undercuts the belief that Jesus is merely a behavior specialist who deserves my allegiance. Observing his life is not intended to collapse into a self-willed mimicking of right choices. Jesus is with me here and now because Jesus' life continues on, and my own life is lived within his. We pray in Jesus' name because he is our hope. We pray in Jesus' name because it is within his life that we now live. We pray in Jesus' name because everything about who we are has changed since he was born for us, died for us, was raised for us, and ascended to God for us.

Standing Before the Father

The reality of our prayers of faith, therefore, is that in Christ we will be known by the Father. When we draw near to God, he will accept us as Christ's. Christ, therefore, is our only hope. Again, the author of Hebrews drew the picture well: "We have this as a sure and steadfast anchor of the soul, a hope that enters into the inner place behind the curtain, where Jesus has gone as a forerunner on our behalf, having become a high priest forever . . ." (6:19–20). The anchor that establishes the foundation of our souls is Christ, who grounds our hope and identity within his person and work. Our identity is out of our hands, so we must unclench them and release all to God. Prayer, true prayer, is the act of opening our hands before the Father and receiving the gift we could not earn. Christ allows us to draw near. Only in the name of Jesus are we ushered before the Lord of glory. You stand before the Father because Christ brought you there. You are raised because Christ died and rose again. You are free because Christ took on the bonds of sin and death and exposed them for what they are. Part of what we are doing in prayer is coming to grips with who we are before the Father as his penetrating gaze undoes us.

As we stand before the Father in Christ, we learn how to pray. As we stand before the Father as dust, we learn to grasp that we are beloved dust. Paul told us, "Our citizenship is in heaven" (Phil. 3:20). Therefore, in prayer we come to acclimate ourselves to the nature of our home. In prayer we come to grasp that the currency of heaven is love. In prayer we learn that the language of heaven is grace. In prayer we learn to harmonize ourselves with the songs of heaven. In prayer we learn, *actually learn*, that "it is finished" (John 19:30). It is only through the life of prayer that we come to earnestly pray, "Abba!"

Life in the Temple

My wife and I (Kyle) woke early to catch the ferry, walking along the beach to the dock as the sun was rising. It was a beautiful day in Oban, Scotland. As we boarded the ferry, we gazed down at the surprisingly crystal-clear water. The water in the region evokes thoughts of the Caribbean more than the murky mist and fog Scotland is known for. Our ferry took us to the Isle of Mull and dropped us off with a large group of other tourists. We climbed aboard our bus and proceeded down a one-lane road across the island to the port on the other side. We were not there to see Mull; we were heading to the famous Iona Abbey. On the other side of the Isle of Mull, we took a boat across the shimmering blue water to Iona.

Iona Abbey was originally founded by Saint Columba in AD 563. To this day it remains a place of pilgrimage for some and tourism for others interested in its history. A new abbey was built to replace the old one, which was tragically destroyed by Vikings. Historic ruins dot the landscape, and Celtic crosses rest all around the abbey grounds. On that warm, summer day there were a lot of people making the trip to see Iona.

As we walked the grounds, inside and outside the abbey, I saw tourists choosing places to pray. I was struck by the distance people had traveled to try to connect with God. There seemed to be a belief that prayer might just work better in that place. People seemed to think that their prayers would finally be heard if they prayed them from there. It was as if the history of the abbey, and the spiritual people who came before them, somehow sanctified their prayers. It was as if the place granted them closer access to God. While I think this belief is misguided, there is something true at the heart of this inclination. However, the place the people were searching for was not an ancient holy site, but Christ. In Christ, we find the place where our prayers are sanctified and brought before the Father. Jesus himself is our sacred space.

Just like the tourists at Iona we convince ourselves that the right time and place will make all the difference in the world in our approach to God. To really grasp our calling in prayer we do indeed have to understand the *where* of prayer. I am not talking about making sure you rise early in the morning to pray or finding a famous cathedral to deliver your most important prayers in. This is not a question of location or technique. I'm referencing where we are led in our prayers. In prayer, we are led to the Father by Christ. Prayer, true prayer, is coming with confidence before the throne of grace; it is standing before the Father in the name of Jesus. We have another who is going before us, speaking on our behalf first. We are brought along as well, with all the confidence and comfort we need in our mediator, Christ Jesus. We do not need to go looking for a sacred space, because we already have one. In this place we are more than tourists; we are welcomed as children in the household of God, at home in the place that is ours. It is there that you bring your life as a sacrifice. It is there that you bring every aspect of your life not conformed to his. Naked, exposed, and vulnerable, you come before the Father with the name of Jesus on your lips.

This is the prayer of faith. This is boldly drawing near to the throne of grace. We have a High Priest who took on dust so that he could tear apart the curtain distancing us from the God of love. "Therefore God has highly exalted him and bestowed on him the name that is above every name, so that at the name of Jesus every knee should bow, in heaven and on earth and under the earth, and every tongue confess that Jesus Christ is Lord, to the glory of God the Father" (Phil. 2:9–11). Standing before the Father in honesty is standing before him in humility. As such, this is a place of rebellion. Paul said, "I would not have known what it is to covet if the law had not said, 'You shall not covet.' But sin, seizing an opportunity through the commandment, produced in me all kinds of covetousness" (Rom. 7:7–8). Similarly, when standing before a holy God, your heart responds based on its nature. The sin that still resides within you breaks out, sometimes in outright rebellion and other times in attempts to hide and cover from the gaze of God. Our hearts might ask us to respond as Peter did when confronted by Christ: "Depart from me, for I am a sinful man, O Lord" (Luke 5:8). Everything that comes out of our hearts in the presence of the Lord is an invitation to be known by him. Whether it is fear, shame, pride, anxiety, or even lust, our call is to open those things before him and receive redemption as those who desperately need it. In prayer we come to fully understand the nature of our redemption; prayer is the place where we become truly known by God.

Learning to be known in prayer is learning to pray in faith. Peter encouraged believers, "Humble yourselves, therefore, under the mighty hand of God so that at the proper time he may exalt you, casting all your anxieties on him, because he cares for you. Be sober-minded; be watchful. Your adversary the devil prowls around like a roaring lion, seeking someone to devour" (1 Peter 5:6–8). The Father cares for you. Your heart will sometimes say otherwise, especially in prayer. Jesus told us that "you will ask in my name, and I do not say to you that I will ask the Father on your behalf; for the Father himself loves you" (John 16:26–27). Again, your heart will say otherwise. Faith is standing before the Father, accepted, because you always stand before him as his own. Faith allows us to claim with John, "for whenever our heart condemns us, God is greater than our heart, and he knows everything" (1 John 3:20). As those in Christ, we are with the Father in Christ's relationship with the Father; "our fellowship is with the Father and with his Son Jesus Christ" (1 John 1:3). We are not strangers in prayer, but are received as beloved.

We need to attend to our hearts in prayer because they unveil the nature of our rebellion and desires to hide. I (Jamin) can remember a man confessing to me that when he entered in to prayer, he frequently ended up fantasizing and lusting much of the time. I could see the guilt and shame in his eyes. He wanted to know how he could fix the problem, how he could make it stop, so that he didn't have to feel bad about himself anymore and he could be reassured God wouldn't be disappointed with him. This is not an uncommon story. It is rarely talked about in the church, but it is experienced by many men in prayer. The truth is that a very high percentage of men are addicted to pornography. A mind saturated with sexual images begins to run wild the moment there is silence. For others who may not struggle with pornography, their minds wander through untold vistas of worry and anxiety the moment they enter prayer. Others simply fall asleep within a few minutes, because they find themselves bored or disinterested. In one way or another, we all encounter our dustiness in prayer.

God isn't calling you to get your act together somewhere else and come back when you are ready to pray "perfectly" (whatever that means). Rather, he is calling you to be who you are before him. God calls out your mind-wandering, sleepiness, lustfulness, greed, anger, and impatience because he sees it for what it is. He calls out all that you are before him, so that you can see it, and utter the name of Christ over it. Prayer is difficult for many because they are still trying to work their way in to God's presence. We work through ways to be accepted by God and to feel okay about ourselves, and so we refuse to be who we really are in our vulnerability. Many, likewise, wrestle to figure out the right way to pray so they may be heard. All of us, to some degree, struggle to grasp how Christ completely changed the nature of prayer. God is calling us here to rest fully in his presence, that in his presence we can live out the life of Jesus in the world.

Prayer in the temple is the prayer of one who has been "naked and exposed to the eyes of him to whom we must give account" (Heb. 4:13). Just as bringing a sacrifice to the temple, this prayer takes time and effort—time and effort that may sometimes feel pointless. Just as having to sacrifice one of the animals that help you survive, sometimes prayer will feel counterproductive because you feel so much of your sinful, fleshly self. Seeing the mess of our hearts rarely feels productive. We want to focus on hearing a new insight from God about our vocations. We want to focus on boldly praying for others and seeing God's answer to our fervent prayers. Just like the disciples who walked out of the temple and proclaimed to Jesus, "Look, Teacher, what wonderful stones and what wonderful buildings!" (Mark 13:1), you might get caught up in things you consider bigger, more impressive, and more important. You may seek for power in prayer, when Christ points to weakness (2 Cor. 12:9). You may want to look at anything but yourself, when in fact that is precisely where he is pointing.

To stand in the temple before our holy God, to be watchful and sober-minded, is to recognize that prayer is much bigger than we imagine. Prayer is not only for meals, church, and bedtime, but incorporates the entirety of our lives. Our call to "pray without ceasing" is to recognize that all life is lived with the Lord (1 Thess. 5:17). Each moment we are called to draw near to God because we live *in* Christ and therefore *in* the temple where his presence resides. Each step of history cascades toward the end of times when God's presence will saturate reality. As God's people, we participate in the inauguration of that time in faith. Christ is with us and in us, and therefore our lives are lived before him. Learning to pray in the temple is learning to live before the face of God. It is practicing the presence of God in everything you do.[8] Every emotion, task, relationship, and event in your life is an invitation to be with the Lord. As we have seen, this was the life that Jesus lived, and we, too, are called to participate in that life.

NINE

THE SILENT EMBRACE //

AFTER JESUS WAS raised from the dead, his sporadic appearances understandably caught the disciples off guard. Jesus' appearances must have seemed surprising and confusing. In a similar manner, Jesus' ascension to the Father was equally bewildering. Luke told us that as the disciples "were gazing into heaven as he went, behold, two men stood by them in white robes, and said, 'Men of Galilee, why do you stand looking into heaven?'" (Acts 1:10–11). As Jesus ascended back to the Father, the disciples stood, no doubt with mouths open, gawking heavenward. The angels admonished them to focus on the task Jesus gave them and not just stand staring. Similarly, I think, many of us are dumbfounded at Jesus' departure and therefore miss its significance. Like the disciples, we easily stare into the heavens wondering why Jesus left. Jesus' promise, "I am with you always, to the end of the age" drifts from our minds (Matt. 28:20). We may hear Jesus' promises of rest and peace, but if we are honest, we often live on other foundations (however slippery and weak). Rather than clutching his promises, we trust in other things. We might nod our heads in approval when we hear we are currently residing in the temple of God, but the worries of the world choke out these truths in our hearts. We want rest, but we turn to escape instead and find restlessness. We want to know peace, but we roll around in the chaos of dustiness. We are unable to rest in the present because we are busy trying to undo the past or control the future.

To close this book, therefore, we turn our attention to real rest and real peace. Everything we have talked about until now points ahead to this truth. Every aspect of who we are and who God is calls us into this rest and peace, but it is often unknown to us. Jonathan Edwards expressed what it looks like to know the peace and rest of God:

> It seemed to me, it [holiness] brought an inexpressible purity, brightness, peacefulness, and ravishment to the soul: and that it made the soul like a field or garden of God, with all manner of pleasant flowers; that is all pleasant, delightful and undisturbed; enjoying a sweet calm, and the gentle vivifying beams of the sun. The soul of a true Christian, as I then wrote my meditations, appeared like such a little white flower, as we see in the spring of the year; low and humble on the ground, opening its bosom, to receive the pleasant beams of the sun's glory; rejoicing as it were, in a calm rapture; diffusing around a sweet fragrancy; standing peacefully and lovingly, in the midst of other flowers round about; all in like manner opening their bosoms, to drink in the light of the sun.[1]

The heart of this image is the Christian in awe of the beauty and glory of God, where the only reasonable response is to bask in the light of his love. In this image, we see the person who has come to know peace and rest in her Lord. She is like a flower who opens to the sun, rejoicing so deeply in the sun that she emits a fragrance of his love. This is an image of the Christian who experiences the love of her Lord. To understand the heart of the Christian life, we have to understand this peace. To understand the heart of prayer, we have to know what it means to "drink in the light of the sun" as the foundation of our prayer lives. To fully grasp the nature of this love, we must come to grips with the notion that Christ has accomplished all.

The Experience of Love

It is hard for us to understand, particularly when we are young in the faith, that Jesus' departure was good for us. Jesus reminded his disciples, "If you loved me, you would have rejoiced, because I am going to the Father, for the Father is greater than I" (John 14:28). Jesus' ascent to the Father broke open God's relational life of love. How so? First, Christ ascended to the Father's presence in our nature, *bringing us* before the Father in himself. Second, Christ sent his Spirit to *draw us* to the God of love. In light of this, we now turn to address one of the key elements in our prayer lives—rest. This is probably not what you think it is—rest is not inaction or laziness. It is not merely the default result of having nothing to do. Rest is the foundation for our lives in God.

When I (Kyle) was a younger man, I remember talking to older married couples about when they met, how they fell in love, and when they knew their spouses were "the one." What fascinated me was that everyone's story ended the same. "There came a point where we *just knew*," they would inevitably say. No one could provide a more detailed or helpful explanation. To someone who is single, that kind of answer is infuriating. It is infuriating, I should add, until you get married yourself and find that same answer on your own lips. When we turn to answers such as "you just know," we are hinting at something incredibly deep in our hearts. It is so deep, in fact, that all we can do is point at it. We tell stories, use metaphors, and sometimes just point and say, "You know," in an attempt to explain something we only really know experientially. Amazingly these things are often the most important and fundamental parts of who we are. When marriage grows deeper with time, love, and discernment, our inability to put words to our unions ceases to bother us. Silence is not necessarily something to overcome, but a sign of an abiding love that speaks for itself. Love binds hearts together to create peace between them. Undergirding the everyday, mundane, and exciting exists a profound comfort with each other, whose presence is like an invisible stability upholding them both in love. Like stones on a riverbed that have conformed to the rushing water, two souls have conformed to fit neatly together in unity. Like the ceaseless flow of the river, the rushing waves of love through time form us so that we are more fitting to our environment—the unity of marriage.

As Paul exposited the depth of love in marriage, he hinted that the profundity of marriage points beyond itself to the union of love the church shares with Christ (Eph. 5:32). The same mysteries we find indescribable in marriage are all the more so in our relationships with God. For many of us, our conversion stories share this same kind of mystery and indescribability. Jonathan Edwards pointed to this reality when he said, "As to a definition of divine love, things of this nature are not properly capable of a definition. They are better felt than defined."[2] When asked about this divine love, we can only utter things such as, "I just knew." In conversion, we become part of the church known as the bride of Christ. Our further growth necessitates our abiding in Christ—he is our love, and we his people. In prayer we come to foster the depth of intimacy possible only through time. Far beyond the insecurity we feel in our relationships with other broken and fallible people, in Christ we can know *real peace* and *real relational depth*. Christ's proclamation that "it is finished" cradles us in our development, as does Paul's proclamation that "there is therefore now no condemnation for those who are in Christ Jesus" (Rom. 8:1). We are cradled in the security of the grace and peace of God, because our grace and peace is ultimately Christ himself. While our knowledge *about* this is secure—"Christ is the solid rock upon which I stand"— our knowledge *of* this reality is had fully only in prayer. This is a truth we must know in prayer with our beloved. As his Spirit binds us to his life, the love we have in him is a formative love. It is the rushing water through us, in us, and for us that harmonizes our hearts with his.

The God Who Prays

Turning back to our image of smooth stones in a riverbed, we must fix our attention on God as a praying God. God's own prayers are the water that rushes over us and through us to conform our hearts to his life of love. God's own prayers pull us in to this relationship to the Father in Christ by the Spirit. Therefore, it is within God's own praying that we pray.

In Romans 8 Paul questioned, "Who shall bring any charge against God's elect?" His response was simple, "Christ Jesus is the one who died—more than that, who was raised—who is at the right hand of God, who indeed is interceding for us" (vv. 33–34). Paul inquired who could possibly charge God's people when we have Christ. But Paul didn't stop there. We not only have Christ, but Christ prays for us. We have already seen that Christ, as our High Priest, intercedes for us. We also know that no one can come to the Father except through Christ (John 14:6). In conversion we have come before the Father as Christ's own, and in prayer we draw near to the Father in Christ. But even more deeply, Jesus has already drawn near to the Father in our stead, and Jesus already draws near to the Father in prayer for us. Christ, our great High Priest, stands in the "presence of God on our behalf" (Heb. 9:24). This is one of the most profound aspects of our own prayer lives, but one that can easily go by unnoticed. *Our prayers rest in God's prayers for us.* Just as we live on borrowed breath, so we pray on borrowed prayer.

We get a glimpse of this in the Gospels as we observe Jesus praying for his disciples. Jesus told Peter, "Behold, Satan demanded to have you, that he might sift you like wheat, but I have prayed for you that your faith may not fail" (Luke 22:31–32). In John 17 we are told that Jesus prayed to the Father for the disciples and opened his prayers up to all his people: "I do not ask for these only, but also for those who will believe in me through their word, that they may all be one, just as you, Father, are in me, and I in you, that they also may be in us, so that the world may believe that you have sent me" (vv. 20–21). Jesus lifted his people up to the Father in prayer, holding them within himself and his faithfulness, grace, and truth. Jesus prayed that we would be "in them," communing with Father and Son in the Spirit of his love. Jesus calls us into his relationship that has eternally existed in the purity of perfect love.

Most of us do not often think about Jesus praying for us. Jesus feels far off, and we feel isolated. Our prayers, we imagine, must make it on their own. Therefore, we are tempted to use a lot of words or make our prayers "better" so that they will work. We think that the right grammar, style, or intensity will guarantee the arrival of our prayers in heaven. This could not be further from the truth. Our prayers rest on the intercession of Jesus. Just as the old married couple no longer explains much about who they are and no longer feels the need to work hard to prove they are valuable, our prayers can come to rest on a deeper and more silent prayer. The old married couple's silence does not point to a lack of communication, but a deep understanding. In light of Jesus' praying before the Father for us, we must come to know a silence before God. Just as there is "a time to speak," there is a "time to keep silence" before the Lord (Eccl. 3:7). This silence is not wasting time, nor is it the awkward silence on a date that signals all is not well; this silence is taking time to rest on the prayers of the Son. In our silent prayers before God, we are uttering "Amen" to the intercession of Jesus. Our call to pray without ceasing is a call to abide in the unceasing prayers of Christ.

This intercession, it should be noted, does not end in the

Son. With the Son, so also with the Spirit. "Likewise the Spirit helps us in our weakness. For we do not know what to pray for as we ought, but the Spirit himself intercedes for us with groanings too deep for words. And he who searches hearts knows what is the mind of the Spirit, because the Spirit intercedes for the saints according to the will of God" (Rom. 8:26–27). In the depths of our hearts, searching out our brokenness, pain, and struggle, the Spirit of God is groaning. What the Spirit experiences and saturates at our core is beyond words. Even God turns to groaning at the profound misery within us. This groaning, it should be said, is not out of hopelessness, but stems from the knowledge of holiness. The Spirit, as God's Spirit, knows and experiences the depths of God's life. It is, in fact, his own life. Likewise, the Spirit knows the depths of your own brokenness and experiences it from the inside. From within us the Spirit prays to the Father on our behalf. What a profound truth this is. God could not be more deeply, more intimately acquainted with all our ways—both speakable and unspeakable. He does not simply know about our ways from the outside, but he knows them from the inside, from deep places in our hearts, un-navigated even by us.

After I (Kyle) got married, I quickly learned that my wife wasn't bringing me her problems because she thought I could fix them. She wasn't interested in sharing her grief, her anxiety, or her fear so that I could rationally explain solutions and correct her emotions. She wanted to be heard. She wanted me to be with her in the midst of her frustrations. With God, we often do the opposite. We want things fixed. We want bad things to go away. Like Paul, we pray that this thorn in our flesh would be taken from us, and Jesus' reply to him is helpful for us as well:

"My grace is sufficient for you, for my power is made perfect in weakness" (2 Cor. 12:9). That weakness is known in silence and rest before God. That weakness is known in being *with* God, truly with him as we are. What we are learning in this weakness—this silence and rest—is to depend on him in all things and for all things. We are learning the posture of dust and coming to embrace it as a gift and blessing.

From within and without, God prays for us. The Spirit pulls God's life of love within our own by investing himself in the deep places of our hearts. We pray in the Spirit as we pray from within this life of love. God's prayers, in other words, provide the context for our own prayers. The words of our prayers don't disturb silence, but enter a conversation about our souls that our triune God is already having. As we saw in the last chapter, the location of our prayers is the temple, within God's own presence. Likewise, and maybe even more profoundly, our prayers take place within God's prayers. As C. S. Lewis noted, "If the Holy Spirit speaks in man, then in prayer God speaks to God."[3] Even now we have the Spirit who is the "guarantee of our inheritance," our down payment, of the future reality of God's perfect presence (Eph. 1:14). In the Spirit we experience, however dimly, that our prayers are caught up by the Spirit within us and sanctified by Christ as he brings them to the Father through his own intercession.

Just as the rocks at the bottom of the stream slowly conform to the contours of the rushing water, so we slowly conform to the rushing groans of the Spirit and the intercessions of Jesus. This is part of God's plan to "tune our hearts to sing his grace," as stated in the great hymn. Just as Jesus comes to pray within the contours of the Psalms and the "joy that was set before him" (Heb. 12:2), so, too, our prayers find their contours through Scripture and the praying life of God. In the silence of resting on God's prayers for us, our hearts become tuned to the grace of God who has called us into his own life. Our hearts come to harmonize with the symphony of Christ as we learn to rest in his work on our behalf.

To understand this harmony, it is helpful to turn to the idea of "sympathetic resonance." Sympathetic resonance is the phenomena of one object responding to and harmonizing with vibrations set off by another object. Take a piano for instance. If you slowly push down a key on a piano, slowly enough so it doesn't play but simply lifts the dampener off the string, you are freeing the string to move. Because nothing is striking it, it doesn't make a noise, but it is free to. If you then strike the key one octave below, you will notice that the one you held down plays as well. The sound you would hear is the result of sympathetic resonance. The more you play the lower octave, the more the other note would play as well. In its freedom, it is harmonizing with the lower octave. The life of the note is received and embraced and creates a life through the passive string as well.[4] Similarly, we are passive as we learn to resonate in response to the prayers of God. God's gift of the Spirit lifts the dampening effects of sin off of our hearts so that we are now free to harmonize with his life—"where the Spirit of the Lord is, there is freedom" (2 Cor. 3:17). We learn to harmonize with the life of Christ as our hearts are conformed to the Spirit's tune within us. We still work—we are not inactive—but our activity is known from within the activity of another: Christ.

God's Life of Love

I (Kyle) once found myself completely exasperated spiritually. After disappointment piled upon disappointment, frustration upon frustration, I was tempted to turn to numbing. I tried to pray, but all I seemed to experience was more of myself. My emotions were too thick, it seemed, to get through to speak with my God. I ended up drowning in the murky water I was hoping to work through. Then, tired and frustrated, I stopped trying to do something about my situation. The only thought that captivated my attention was that God knows, understands, and guides. Even my frustrations, I thought to myself, can be used for the good of those who love him (Rom. 8:28). In that moment I ceased striving to fix, create, and redeem on my own; I simply sat in silence with my God. In that day I knew the presence and sustenance of the Lord.

In Christ we draw near to the Father. And by the intercession of Son and Spirit, we are lifted up to the Father as we really are, in ways unknown even to us, and are offered to him in spirit and truth. It is within God's own life of prayer that our "drawing near" comes into its own. Only as we come to grasp that we draw near because he draws near to us, do we enter into the depths of prayer. We did not initiate salvation, but God first loved us (1 John 4:19) and sent his Son to us when we were still sinners (Rom. 5:8). So, too, in prayer do we enter the presence of the God who has invited us, called us, and even entered into our own souls, praying from our depths. We rest in the work God has done, but that rest isn't inactivity or laziness, it is a new kind of calling standing on the foundation of God's own life of love.

Many people fail to embrace the truth that it was in their sins that Christ died for them, and that in him there is now no condemnation (Rom. 8:1). By failing to internalize Christ's work, prayer is turned into a place to be good, or, more likely, a place to pretend you are good. Prayer, in this sense, is restless and vain.

Entering God's Rest

Rest is never fully known now because we do not reside in the full presence of God. We only know communion with God through a glass darkly. Paul told us that "we know that the whole creation has been groaning together in the pains of childbirth until now. And not only the creation, but we ourselves, who have the firstfruits of the Spirit, groan inwardly as we wait eagerly for adoption as sons and daughters, the redemption of our bodies" (Rom. 8:22–23).[5] We groan as we feel the weight of death in our bodies—the dust calling us back to itself as our bodies cease to function well. The more life we experience, and the more of ourselves we experience, the more groaning becomes the deep cry of our hearts. We rest in God as we walk through this groaning. We should not avoid this groaning or treat it with contempt as unspiritual or immature. Rather, it is our calling. To grow in our prayer lives we must grow in our ability to pray in the posture of groaning, sometimes without words at all, holding our hands open before the Father of love as one who is upheld in the prayers of Son and Spirit. Sometimes, with David, we must recognize that even our capacity to lie down and sleep is the Lord's sustenance (Ps. 3:5). We can lie down and sleep in Jesus' name, knowing rest in his sustaining grace.

Throughout the history of redemption the Lord has been calling his people to rest in him. From the promised land to Jesus' call to Jerusalem, "How often would I have gathered your children together as a hen gathers her brood under her wings" (Luke 13:34), the Lord is calling his people to himself. Faith in Christ is being gathered together under Christ's wings, resting in him to know his grace, provision, and sustaining power. The key moment of this, for us, is conversion: "There remains a Sabbath rest for the people of God, for whoever has entered God's rest has also rested from his works as God did from his" (Heb. 4:9–10). We are told to "strive to enter that rest" (Heb. 4:11). God's rest is Christ himself; that is where our hope resides. Christ himself is our "wisdom from God, righteousness and sanctification and redemption" (1 Cor. 1:30). Christ is our rest. Just as we lay down our works to grasp fully onto the rest of God, so, too, in prayer do we lay down all we have to rest in Christ and his prayers on our behalf. This is most fully understood only when we can come before the Lord in utter silence, not seeking to justify ourselves, prove ourselves, make excuses for ourselves, or even announce our presence. In the presence of the Lord, we rest in the intercession of the Son and Spirit. In the presence of the Lord, we draw near based on what the Lord has already done for us. There, before the face of God, we find rest and peace in the work of another. Just like the old couple whose silence sings loud exaltations of a life lived in communion, so, too, our silence shouts praise. In this silence we come to know what the Lord means when he commands, "Be still, and know that I am God" (Ps. 46:10). In his presence and in our silence, we can be dust before our Creator, seeking to be nothing more or less than his beloved.

Just as we boldly approached the throne of grace in confidence, not in ourselves but in Christ, so, too, we boldly approach God as one who has already been approached by God. We do not enter in unannounced, but are introduced into the prayer life of God by Christ and his indwelling Spirit. Our God is the God who abides in us (1 John 4:15), and that abiding grounds our abiding in Christ (John 15:4). Christ is "able to save to the uttermost those who draw near to God through him, since he always lives to make intercession for them" (Heb. 7:25). In this we proclaim, "All is from you, through you and to you, to you be glory forever and ever" (Rom. 11:36, paraphrased). By casting ourselves on the prayers of God, our cries to be his come to fruition. Here, in resting on the work of God and not ourselves, we come to grasp our call to relate in the freedom he provides rather than in the bonds of our flesh. When we are caught up in God's movement of praying for us, in us, and through us, we are free.

We are free to love others and not use them, because we are no longer the center of our universe, but find ourselves in orbit around Christ.

We are free to rest in God's grace.

We are free to know and be known because God has made himself known to us in Christ.

In this freedom we can finally allow ourselves to be known in prayer, and to know the God of love as he cascades his prayers over us. Before the face of the Lord we know freedom, freedom to live in him, and freedom to set our minds on him that we may be formed in his image: "Now the Lord is the Spirit, and where the Spirit of the Lord is, there is freedom. And we all, with unveiled face, beholding the glory of the Lord, are being transformed into the same image from one degree of glory to another. For this comes from the Lord who is the Spirit" (2 Cor. 3:17–18). The Spirit who prays in us and through us unveils the Lord of glory to our hearts, catching our complete attention by the beauty of his grace.

Likewise, in this prayer of silence we come to pray, not for ourselves, but simply come to *be with* our God. In the words of the Psalmist, "For a day in your courts is better than a thousand elsewhere" (Ps. 84:10). In this kind of prayer you bring your whole self to lay before God, as if you were bringing an animal to sacrifice for your sins. You are saying, "I am yours, take me." But in doing so, there is a certain and important self-forgetfulness.[6] You come to the Lord because he is your love, not because he might answer your prayers or because you need guidance (as important as those are), but because he is God. In his grace your heart stretches out fully to him so you can forget yourself. Just as majestic beauty can so captivate your imagination that the worries of your life and your current situation seem to fade away, so, too, in the prayer of silence does all else seem insignificant. What you are doing in this prayer is ceasing to worry about your life, trusting that God knows every hair on your head (Matt. 10:30). What you are doing is grasping a healthy self-forgetfulness, trusting that God remembers you, so you don't have to. What you are doing is fully embracing that you are dust, while at the same time resting in the truth that you are God's beloved.

The prayer of silence is coming before God and trusting. It is trusting that Christ's promises are real and his precepts true. The whole structure beneath the silence is filled with words—with promises, admonitions, discipline, and truth; with love, hope, and knowledge of each other. It is the prayer of a sheep who knows the shepherd's voice, and therefore rests silently in the calming reassurance of his call. The breadth of everything God has given you is wielded fully in silence. Beneath this trust rests the knowledge that he will never leave us or forsake us (Heb. 13:5–6) and that he is with us always, even to the end of the age (Matt. 28:20). Beneath this trust is the truth that, "The LORD your God is in your midst, a mighty one who will save; he will rejoice over you with gladness; he will quiet you by his love; he will exult over you with loud singing" (Zeph. 3:17). The Lord quiets us by his love, and our silence is the response to knowing love that is beyond understanding (Eph. 3:19). As such, the prayer of silence is what all prayers work toward and what all prayers build on. It fuels prayer because it is the fruit of God's self-given communion, love, and grace. We come to know this silence first in conversion, as we kneel at the cross, but it is a silence that grows with us as we rest on the faithfulness of God.

This prayer of rest and silence fuels unceasing prayer (1 Thess. 5:17). Paul's call to pray without ceasing is a continual living of life in the presence of God. It is holding yourself and everyone you meet in that presence, responding and resonating to the prayers of Son and Spirit in us and through us. It is the prayer of the heart that is in harmony with the ways of God. In a broadly similar way, this prayer is like the subconscious awareness we have of certain things around us, like our cell phones. We stand in constant awareness of our cell phones, and most of us would know immediately if it was not in our pockets. That awareness is similar to unceasing prayer. It is not something at the front of your mind, but in the recesses of your consciousness, you are standing before God and offering him everything you are conscious of. What might be a better example is becoming a parent for the first time. Even when you are asleep, which is rare enough, you have another level of consciousness that is listening and attending to your new child. As a relatively new father myself, I (Kyle) find that I continually hold my little children in my thoughts even when I am not directly thinking about them. I often do the same with them in prayer, holding them before the Father in hope. Therefore, praying without ceasing is not a technique. It is not something you can learn to do in five easy steps. Rather, praying without ceasing is the fruit of a spirit at rest, a spirit in love, and therefore is carried along by the receiving and abiding prayers of Son and Spirit for you and in you.

The prayer of silence, what we might call the prayer of rest, occurs in the freedom of the Spirit. It is not self-generated, created in our own efforts through our techniques, but is known as we set our minds on Christ seated at the right hand of God. We have already seen that Christ ushers us into the holy place in the presence of the Father, not naked, but clothed in his righteousness. Furthermore, we come into the Father's presence mid-conversation, carried along by the prayers of the Son and Spirit. It is here where we come to rest. This rest becomes the backdrop to all our activity, all our prayers, such that they flow forth from us not out of chaos, but out of our peace in the Lord. This prayer grounds our identity, such that our prayers and praise become one. The prayer of silence, in this sense, is not the goal, but it fuels the goal of communion with God. The strange concepts of "praying without ceasing" and praying "in the Spirit" are ultimately united in the rest we know as we stand before the Father in Christ. This is the reality of our faith—that we know ourselves as those held in God's presence in Christ. We pray without ceasing in the Spirit when we live from that place, and hold ourselves open before the God who prays from within. In our silence and openness to the Spirit we are the piano string waiting to harmonize with God through the resonance of the Spirit within.

Walking Forward in Silence

Jesus told a parable of two pray-ers:

> Two men went up into the temple to pray, one a Pharisee and
> the other a tax collector. The Pharisee, standing by himself,
> prayed thus: "God, I thank you that I am not like other men,
> extortioners, unjust, adulterers, or even like this tax collector.
> I fast twice a week; I give tithes of all that I get." But the tax
> collector, standing far off, would not even lift up his eyes to
> heaven, but beat his breast, saying, "God, be merciful to me,
> a sinner!" I tell you, this man went down to his house justi-
> fied, rather than the other. For everyone who exalts himself
> will be humbled, but the one who humbles himself will be
> exalted. (Luke 18:10–14)

The prayer of silence is a spiritual manifestation of what the tax collector was doing when he prayed. The tax collector knew the truth of himself when he prayed to God. He easily could have multiplied his words as the Pharisee, but chose not to. His terseness cuts to his heart without apology or camouflage. In a similar way, the prayer of silence is not an attempt to avoid communication. Every murmur under the surface of your heart, all the emotion that runs deeper than words, is only fully held before the Father in silence. The prayer of silence taps in to the posture of all prayer, falling on your knees with open hands and heart before the God of glory. This prayer is reverently opening yourself to the truth of who you are, truths you know you don't fully grasp, as God himself searches you and knows you (Ps. 139:23–24). This prayer is a continual "Amen" to Jesus' and the Spirit's prayers within us—an "Amen" to Christ's words, "It is finished."

Praying in silence is often done in one of two main forms: praying in silence out of desperation, and practicing the prayer of silence. You may have prayed the prayer of silence in your own desperation without realizing it or naming it as such. Many people are led into this prayer through tragedy, anxiety, fear, or simply being overwhelmed by their sins and wondering why God hasn't "fixed things." This is not a praying that you practice for, nor is it something you generate on your own; this is simply doing the only thing you can because words cannot express the truth of your heart. The Spirit groans in our hearts because words cannot express our brokenness (Rom. 8:26), and therefore we come in silence because words cannot express the truth of our pain. The second form of praying in silence is practicing silence. This *is* something we practice, because silence is an important posture of our hearts before God. Briefly, let me narrate these two realities.

THE SILENCE OF DESPERATION

I (Kyle) have a friend who walked through what every parent fears: the diagnosis that their little daughter had cancer. After many months of hospital visits and with good news finally on the horizon, we talked on the phone. Something he said struck me as important. He explained that in this season of their lives, they had less time than ever to spend focused time with God. They were spending less time in Scripture than they normally did, and less time set aside for prayer than there normally was. And yet, in this time, he explained, they felt the presence and grace of God more fully than ever before. This often occurs when people suffer. In ways we will never fully understand, our suffering triggers prayer beneath the surface of our hearts and consciousness. This is the prayer of silence. At times, without us even knowing it, we are resting on God in silence. This silence may come in the midst of chaos. This silence carries us along, and only when we stop and let the silence overtake us do we even realize it is there. At the core of our beings God ministers to us. In the depths of our hearts his presence saturates our misery. Beneath our own groaning, God is groaning with us. We don't groan alone, aching to be heard, but rather groan with God who knows the source of our hearts' rumble more deeply than we do ourselves. Faced with the hopelessness our pain often brings us, we hold our groans before the Lord in silence knowing that he is our only hope. In that hope we rest in the fact that every tear will be wiped away, all our hunger satisfied, and we will be shepherded by the Lamb who bore our sins.

While suffering can usher us into the prayer of silence, we should not simply wait for suffering to do so. The reason suffering wakes us to this kind of prayer is that we are deafened by our desperate need for excitement. We have come to think that growth in the Christian life is always linked to a felt experience of God or an experience of excitement. This is a form of the "prosperity gospel," where God will bless us financially if we have faith, but now God is blessing us with excitement. Silence to our culture, on the other hand, is akin to death. To a culture that is always connecting with words and images from our phones, computers, and billboards, silence overwhelms us. This is why it takes something like pain, misery, or a tragedy to allow for this silence. We need a break from the fantasy world of noise we believe is reality. In the noise of our lives, with the belief that excitement is the cure-all aid for our souls, it is only silence that can help us rest on the real foundation—the prayers of the Son and the Spirit in us, through us and for us. Those prayers are the rushing water that nourishes and forms us, slowly but distinctly, into the image of the Son who lived life and suffered in the presence of his Father.

PRACTICING THE PRAYER OF SILENCE

Whereas many of us have been forced into the prayer of silence because of our life circumstances, most of us have never practiced silence. It feels lazy. It feels counterproductive. It feels like I'm just wasting my time. But this is the whole point. Silence reveals a heart that desperately wants to self-identify with productivity and accomplishment. Silence reveals a heart that wants to use God to feel a certain way. Silence reveals a heart that is more interested assuaging its guilt than being with God. In silence, these realities come to the surface quickly; it has a way of calling forth our idolatrous images of God and exposing them. In these times, we will always be tempted to turn to words. As we are experiencing the truth of ourselves, truths that embarrass us and fill us with shame, we often turn to words as a way to self-justify. Maybe we pray for other people, not because we care for them, but because doing so makes us feel better. Maybe we find a new program of praying, so that praying the *right* way allows us to feel more accomplished at prayer. Maybe we turn to confession, using as many words as possible to show God we are repentant, and therefore use those words as a way to feel better about ourselves. Notice the theme. We often turn to words in prayer to feel a certain kind of way and to manipulate our standing before God. We often use words in the way Adam and Eve used fig leaves—to hide.

Perhaps the most difficult thing to accept as a Christian is that our devotion is the place where our rejection of God is revealed. It is in our devotion that we strategically hide from God by being good, dutiful, or savvy. Like the older son in the parable of the two sons, we work hard to do the right things, but never really embrace our identities as children of the Father. Instead, we take on the name of a child, all the while allowing our hearts to slowly die as servants. We turn to practice silence because there we cannot justify ourselves, but rest on the justification of another. In silence we do not rest in our ability to talk our way out of our sins, as Adam tried to do with God (Gen. 3:12), but trust that God's penetrating Word cuts to the core of our hearts leaving us naked and exposed, only to be clothed in his grace (Heb. 4:12–13). As our hearts beg us to speak, they are begging us to hide. In that space, our silence proclaims the posture of Jesus: "Not my will, but yours, be done" (Luke 22:42).

Silence recognizes the limits to our words, and forces us to rest in the words of another. As we experience much of ourselves in silence, our anxious desire to pray something that sounds profound, our desire to come up with something that will hide and cover us from the exposing presence of God, or the more simple (but equally devious) desire to have an experience rather than to have God himself, we are given an opportunity to really be *with* God as we truly are. This silence is handing over our whole selves to the Father, even as the Spirit calls out from our depths and the Son claims us as his. When we do speak, as we hold our hearts up to God, we often need to speak into our own hearts: "Why are you cast down, O my soul?" (Ps. 42:5). It is here, as we turn our soul to God, refusing to hide behind our words, eloquence, or devotion, that we should know the truth proclaimed by the Psalmist: "Deep calls to deep at the roar of your waterfalls; all your breakers and your waves have gone over me" (Ps. 42:7). In this silent place of communion with God who has done all things to redeem us, we trust that the Lord carries us along in his prayers for us, in us, and through us.

Resting on God

As we pray in the presence of God, and as our prayers are carried along by God's prayers, we stand in silent adoration before our God. Here our rest is grounded in hope. In this sense, our prayers mimic the scene John narrated about those who come out of the Great Tribulation:

> They have washed their robes and made them white in the blood of the Lamb. Therefore they are before the throne of God, and serve him day and night in his temple; and he who sits on the throne will shelter them with his presence. They shall hunger no more, neither thirst anymore; the sun shall not strike them, nor any scorching heat. For the Lamb in the midst of the throne will be their shepherd, and he will guide them to springs of living water, and God will wipe away every tear from their eyes. When the Lamb opened the seventh seal, there was silence in heaven for about half an hour. (Rev. 7:14–8:1)

Our prayers and lives are formed in this silence. In the presence of God we stand confidently before the throne of grace, silently uttering, "Here I am, I am yours." In these moments desperation is laid aside, our struggles dissipate, and our frustrations cease. Here, in these moments, we not only set our minds on things above, but set our very lives on these things. Here we look to Jesus, "the founder and perfecter of our faith, who for the joy that was set before him endured the cross" (Heb. 12:2). Here, in his presence, we have a bird's-eye view of our lives. Everything we bring before God here, to lay at his feet, is made known. Our desires reveal fleshliness, our frustrations reveal greed, and our hopes often prove misguided. In the silence God invites us to hear things we were not previously listening for. Nonetheless, we draw near, seeking nothing other than Christ and the life he provides.

Conclusion

We must pray not simply shouting out to a God who might hear the echoes of our calls, or who might turn a near-deaf ear to us if we are loud enough. We must come and present ourselves before God, learning in our silence to resonate with the prayers of Son and Spirit. Our request is simple: "Teach me to pray; may you yourself pray in me and through me."[7] In this, we pray without ceasing, living every moment in the presence of God. In this our hearts come to harmonize with his. We come in silence with hope and trust, knowing he will carry us along by his Spirit. Like those who laid down palm branches, shouting, "Hosanna to the Son of David! Blessed is he who comes in the name of the Lord! Hosanna in the highest!" anticipating the arrival of their king, we anticipate when peace reigns and the cries of our hearts are quieted by his love (Matt. 21:9). In our silence we abide in God, and in this silence we come to rest in the way of the cross—the way of weakness—in the world (2 Cor. 12:9). In this weakness the current of silence in our hearts spurs us on in prayers of all kinds and orients our hearts to rest in Christ who has accomplished all. This silence is the fuel for interceding for others, casting our cares on the Lord, and all kinds of word-filled praying. Silence nourishes these prayers, so that they are prayers of faithfulness and not prayers of deceit.

AFTERWORD:
CARVING OUT SPACE
TO BE WITH GOD //

I (KYLE) REMEMBER coming to the realization that I didn't believe in prayer. I was in college, and I had established myself as a spiritual leader on campus. I was a biblical studies student, an RA in my dorm, a chapel speaker, a spiritual mentor, and a Bible tutor. I had done everything I thought I was supposed to do to be mature, and yet I knew otherwise. One evening I was alone in my dorm room reflecting on my spiritual journey, and I started thinking about prayer. *I don't pray much*, I thought to myself. It was then that the big question popped in my head: *If I don't pray, can I really say that I believe in prayer?* The answer I could not avoid was no. It was simply impossible. What would it mean to believe that the God of the universe is with me, listening, attending, and caring for me, and yet never get around to praying?

I had become the older brother in the parable of the two sons. I had fallen victim to the great temptation for Christians: I had embraced the identity of a Christian without ever embracing God. I played the role so well that I was praised for it and put in positions of leadership because of it. But when it was unveiled, I was undone. When I finally saw the truth of my heart, I was able to see what a sham my so-called maturity really was. I wanted more. I wanted God, and I realized that my heart grabbed onto everything but him because it was afraid to be seen and afraid to be known. I was hiding behind my devotion, and God was calling me out of hiding.

I decided to tell a friend of mine that I didn't believe in prayer. I knew that might be embarrassing and potentially awkward, but it was such a profound realization that I had to share it. When I told him that the only way to believe in prayer is to do it, and that I didn't really pray much, I was shocked at his response. "Yeah, I don't either." Together, we decided to tell someone else, who said the same thing, and then again, and again, and again. At a Christian college, among mostly biblical studies students, I found very little prayer going on. We had uncovered an epidemic. We found a lot of people trying to deal with their sins, a lot of people trying really hard to be good (and failing), and a lot of people desperate for abundant life but not finding any. We were all giving ourselves to things that made us feel more mature, but prayer seemed desolate. Prayer wasn't what we wanted it to be, and we had become convinced that we were the problem.

I have no doubt that this isn't an isolated reality. Everywhere I go people share similar stories about their prayer lives (or lack thereof). We've been given a narrow and shallow view of the Christian life, and with it, a superficial understanding of prayer. Rather than finding freedom to be *with* God, we are bound by our own expectations and desires. We embrace a way of trying hard to be good, instead of being embraced by the God who is love. We hunt for an experience of God rather than seeking God himself. We try to prove we are valuable rather than admitting that without him we can do nothing (John 15:5). We readily identify ourselves as Christian but hesitate to really know ourselves as children of the Father.

Throughout this book, we have walked through the truth of ourselves and the truth of what God has done for us. That was the path both Jamin and I had to take after realizing that our spiritual maturity was a ruse. Our goal for this book is that you would learn to walk through the truth of yourself and the truth of God to embrace a deeper calling—the call to be holy. Holiness is not something you do, nor is it something you generate. Holiness is partaking in God's life and being caught up in the love of God (2 Peter 1:4). Holiness is the way of being with the God who is always with you, because you do not merely walk alongside God, but are wrapped up in his life in the Son by the Spirit.

The big question, of course, is what now? What does it mean to embrace our finitude and temporality, our weakness and our brokenness, not in an attempt to fix ourselves (self-help), but to be with God? When we looked at the parable of the two sons, we noted that the Father clothed his prodigal son, allowing the son to partake in the life of the family. He put a family robe around his son's shoulders so that the son could participate in that life. Likewise, when Adam and Eve were naked and ashamed, they tried to hide and cover by clothing themselves, but their strategies for doing so were futile and self-serving. In response, God provided clothes for them, carving out space for them to be with each other without shame, and to be with him without guilt. In Christ, we are given clothes that carve out space for us to be with God and with one another—to love God and love neighbor as ourselves. It is not surprising, in light of this, that when Paul talked about living the virtuous Christian life, one of the key images he turned to was clothing:

> Do not lie to one another, seeing that you have put off the old self with its practices and have put on the new self, which is being renewed in knowledge after the image of its creator. . . . Put on then, as God's chosen ones, holy and beloved, compassionate hearts, kindness, humility, meekness, and patience, bearing with one another and, if one has a complaint against another, forgiving each other; as the Lord has forgiven you, so you also must forgive. And above all these put on love, which binds everything together in perfect harmony. (Col. 3:9–10, 12–14)

We are to "put off" our old ways of life and "put on" the new. As we have seen, being clothed is creating space to be with God and others, and in this sense, love is the great article of clothing that "binds everything together" in harmony. Putting on love is creating space to be united to another in truth and goodness. But one might easily take this as advice to try harder. One might easily presuppose that "putting on" and "putting off" are somehow just doing it. Clothing, after all, is not an essential part of who we are, but things we take on and off easily. If we read this as self-help, all it means is that we are supposed to pretend. Pretend to be humble. Pretend to love. Pretend to have an experience of God in an attempt to make it happen. With enough pretending, one day it might magically be true. But this is not the call of the Christian. Our putting on and off of virtue is moving forward in life with God such that we are not pretending, but allowing all our vices and our attempts at virtue to open us to the truth of ourselves as those who are caught up in the life of God. Notice the major context for Paul's discussion of putting on and off:

> If then you have been raised with Christ, seek the things that
> are above, where Christ is, seated at the right hand of God.
> Set your minds on things that are above, not on things that
> are on earth. For you have died, and your life is hidden with
> Christ in God. When Christ who is your life appears, then
> you also will appear with him in glory. (Col 3:1–4)

Your life is hidden with Christ in God. Seek the things that are above, not the things that are below. This is not leading us into an equation for pretending, but for resting in the truth of ourselves as those redeemed by God.

Therefore, the call to virtue, love, humility, compassion, kindness, gentleness, and self-control are not commands to try harder and be better, but are invitations to live with God. As we press into these callings in our relationships, the truth of our hearts is broken open, and we realize that we don't believe in prayer, or that we are deeply angry, self-righteous, prideful, etc. Clothing yourself in love, humility, or gentleness is to carve out space in the truth of yourself to be with God. To be with the God who is always with you, *you* actually have to be with God. You cannot create an identity of someone who really loves if you do not love. If you are deeply angry, then the only way to come to God in the truth of yourself is to come to him as the one who is deeply angry. To help provide a brief framework for this, let me suggest a way forward. To close, I have three suggestions and encouragements for your journey with God.

Pay Attention to Your Life

First, you need to pay careful attention to how you handle struggles, disappointments, and challenges in the Christian life. When you hear a sermon or read a Bible verse on humility, do you set up a self-help program to be more humble? Do you jump from one program to another year after year, trying to find the right formula to fix your spiritual life? Or, maybe you find yourself giving up because you have tried everything already and nothing seems to work. Rather than concealing the truth, allow the Spirit of God to expose what is really going on. Not only do we tend to hide these things from God and others, but in fact we tend to hide them from ourselves. We all are tempted to live on the surface of life, avoiding the deep things of our souls. God is calling you to pay attention to these aspects of your life and to see through them into the broken truth of your heart. He is calling you into reality, in love.

Here you will be assessing all the various things you do as a Christian. There are two cautions we must offer before you dive in. First, be careful, this is not a self-assessment process. You are not alone trying to figure out your life so that you can feel better about yourself or work on yourself. Rather, you are seeking to discern the truth about who you are before God, by attending to the Spirit's guidance and wisdom, so that you might present yourself to God. Don't just think about your life, but allow the Spirit to unveil the truth of yourself, so you can hold that open before the mercy and grace of God. There is a big difference between these two; prayer should never be self-reflection, but entails holding yourself open before God. Second, be wary of the temptation to fix yourself because you feel guilty. This is not a time to beat yourself up for not being more mature. God is not looking down on you with disdain. Rather, he is with you in love. As you engage in this process of prayerful reflection, don't forget God knows you fully and loves you unconditionally. He is not condemning you, but rather calling you to receive his love in the truth of who you are.

As you begin, be very practical. You may want to write these things down or even process with another person who knows your life well. As you pay attention to your life, you will explore things like your focused times of prayer, church attendance, reading the Bible, giving money, commitment to service or missions work, etc. As you explore each area of your spiritual life, take each one and prayerfully consider a few questions. "Why do I do this?" "How am I experiencing this practice?" "Am I practicing this discipline in order to be with God or rather to fix myself or to have a particular experience?" You might discover that you actually feel fatigued and burdened by the need to have a "daily quiet time." Rather than being life-giving, it feels like another "should" in your life that is disconnected from relationship with God. Or maybe you will identify the feeling of loneliness that you often have in prayer. Perhaps it has been there for a while, but you have been scared to acknowledge it, and now the Spirit is inviting you to be known in that place in love. Perhaps you will discover that you focus solely on certain spiritual disciplines while avoiding others. Maybe what the Spirit is revealing here is a fear to truly dive deep into community because of the vulnerability it entails. Or perhaps you have a desire to focus solely on the discipline of service because it makes you feel like you are a "good person."

What do these patterns and movements in your spiritual life tell you about where you are in your relationship with God? I want you to press deeply into the truth of what your practices tell you about your heart. Remember, the goal is not to roll around in our guilt and shame as we do this, but rather to present ourselves to our loving God in truth. We need to dive deeply into our motivations if we are going to catch a glimpse of the aspects of our souls that God wants to redeem, renew, and re-create. Our calling is to put on virtue, not as clothing to hide, but as being wrapped up in God's life of love. Holiness is always a movement into the truth of God's life in the truth of yourself.

Reframe Your Practices

Next, I would like you to hold in your mind all those activities, prayerfully considering the question: "What would it look like to do this *with* the God who is always with me?" Spiritual practices can easily become idols when they are no longer centered on the goal of abiding. Too often we see them as things we engage in to fix ourselves. Too often accomplishing the particular spiritual discipline is the goal in and of itself. We gauge success based on frequency, focus, and felt experience. This is the trap of the older brother, who focused so intently on being dutiful that he failed to embrace his identity as a son. When we engage in spiritual practices, we are most fundamentally not practicing a certain behavior, but rather a certain relational posture. We are practicing abiding. We abide in the life of God as we abide with Christ by his Spirit. To grasp the notion of abiding we must imbibe Jesus' declaration, "Apart from me you can do nothing" (John 15:5). We do have a role to play in our growth. It is imperative that we do something. God has called us to present ourselves as living sacrifices (Rom. 12:1). But what is most important is the posture we have before God in the midst of our actions. We need to allow our actions to break open space to be with God in the reality of our lives—regardless of what that reality is. No life is too ugly for the beautifying gaze of God. It was in your sin that he died for you (Rom. 5:8), and in him, there is now no condemnation (Rom. 8:1). Know the freedom that Christ provides, not by becoming dutiful, but by abiding in him as the God who is already with you in all things.

Enter Honestly into Life with God

This last point has already been hinted at in the first two. As we reframe our practices around being with God, *you* are the one who must be with God. You cannot send the "you" you only wish existed. You cannot hide from God by being with him as someone other than who you really are. *You* have to be there. Real relationship requires it. To relate to God in the honesty of yourself, your heart must be exposed to God, and you must be *that* person with him. Are you angry? Be the angry person before the face of God. Are you prideful? Be the person filled with pride before God. Are you selfish? Be the selfish person before God. It does not help to pretend you are otherwise. You are not fooling God. To be formed by God necessitates *both* knowing God and knowing oneself in relation to God. You cannot know yourself truly until you know yourself, your true self, as the one who has been redeemed by God. Until you hear the Lord name you his child, in the depths of your heart, you will inevitably work hard to be faithful, rather than working within the faithfulness of God. We do not have to be afraid of our sins before God, because we do not stand before God on the basis of our own intrinsic value. We stand before God on the basis of *his* value and *his* work, and as we are clothed with Christ, we are ushered into the life of God on Christ's behalf. It is here that we can really know that "there is now no condemnation," because only by being embraced by God can we embrace the truth that we are his.

When we take the risk of being honest with God in prayer, we open ourselves up to encounter God's love in the deep places of our souls. When we show up as our true selves, we begin to discover real relationship with the Creator of the universe. We come to know what it is to be known. We cannot encounter God's love if we are not honest, because it is in honesty that we discover a depth of being known that transcends all other relationships in our lives. We also come to know our true selves in the process. We come to know ourselves as those who are redeemed. Thus, as we engage in our spiritual practices, we want these to be places of relational encounter. We want to open our lives to the transforming love of God. Undoubtedly, you will still find yourself worrying about work as you sing praise songs in church, or even lusting in the middle of your Bible reading. Remember, all these things point to the murky depths of one's heart, places heavily guarded by guilt and shame. But it was in these places that Christ died for you. So, you need not worry about being honest. Christ died for you with full knowledge of your rebellion (Rom. 5:8). He died for the real you, the messed-up, sinful, broken, anxious you. Why are you hiding from him now?

Our hope is that this book will serve as an extended meditation on the truth of ourselves in light of the truth of God. We realize that much has been exposed in your heart during the process of reading this book, and that can feel a bit overwhelming. Remember, it will be a journey. This book is not something that can be read and put away, but needs to be chewed on, mulled over, and talked about. You do not generate the Christian life. You do not generate prayer. You are called into the life of prayer God has for you, through you, and in you. You do not know how to pray as you ought (Rom. 8:26), so God has wrapped you up in his life of love. We hope that this book spurs you on, wherever the Lord has you, in the truth of his love for you.

That a man once born should arrive at that life, where
he shall never die. This is what we believe with a heart
well cleansed, cleansed, I mean, of the world's dust; that
this dust close not up our eye of faith.

—AUGUSTINE

That flesh is but the glass, which holds the dust
That measures all our time; which also shall
Be crumbled into dust.

—GEORGE HERBERT

Love is the person of the resurrection, scooping up the
dust and chanting, "Live."

—EMILY DICKINSON

ACKNOWLEDGMENTS //

THIS PROJECT WAS slow in coming. We wrestled through the purpose of this book for more than a year before deciding on the basic themes. Throughout that time, there were many key people who read drafts, spoke into this project, and guided it along the way. Our agent Jenni Burke, who has been such a great support, was an important voice as we were writing. Joel Miller and his team at Thomas Nelson have shown nothing but excitement about this project, and we appreciate your work and passion for what we are doing. We are grateful for the support we have received from our primary places of ministry, Saddleback Church and Biola University. They both have provided much encouragement and excitement for this project, and for that we are grateful. Rick Warren, in particular, has proven to be a constant encouragement for us both, especially in times when encouragement was hard to find. Janet Lee was gracious enough to work through the manuscript twice, giving important feedback and gracious support along the way. Several other people, whose insights we sought out, were kind enough to read chapters here and there, including Michelle Doerr, Jen Manglos, Robby Boyd, Bob Mehaffey, Sam Paschall, and Julie Barrios. Our wives, Kelli and Kristin, have, of course, carried much of the burden of reading early drafts, sifting through ideas, and attending to us as we spoke out loud about our dreams and desires for this book. We are both blessed to have wives so encouraging, who carried the extra burden of creating space for us to take on this project. Thank you so much for your support and love in this process. We are deeply blessed.

NOTES //

CHAPTER 1

1. Eugene Peterson, *Tell It Slant: A Conversation on the Language of Jesus in His Stories and Prayers* (Grand Rapids: Wm B. Eerdmans Publishing, 2008), 161.

2. Gregory of Nyssa, "On the Origin of Man," in *Ancient Christian Commentary on Scripture: Genesis 1–11*, ed. Andrew Louth (Downers Grove: InterVarsity Press, 2001), 28. Gregory of Nyssa stated, "This same language was not used for (the creation) of other things. The command was simple when light was created; God said, 'Let there be light.' Heaven was also made without deliberation . . . These, though, were before (the creation of) humans. For humans, there was deliberation. He did not say, as he did when creating other things, 'Let there be a human.' See how worthy you are! Your origins are not in an imperative. Instead, God deliberated about the best way to bring to life a creation worthy of honor."

3. John Calvin, *Calvin's Commentaries, Genesis*, trans. Rev. John King, vol. 1. (Grand Rapids: Baker Books, 2003), 111. Calvin stated, "He now explains what he had before omitted in the creation of man, that his body was taken out of the earth. He

had said that he was formed after the image of God. This is incomparably the highest nobility; and, lest men should use it as an occasion of pride, their first origin is placed immediately before them; whence they may learn that this advantage was adventitious; for Moses relates that man had been, in the beginning, dust of the earth. Let foolish men now go and boast of the excellency of their nature!"

4. John Walton, *Genesis*, The NIV Application Commentary (Grand Rapids: Zondervan, 2001), 148.

5. John Walton, "Garden of Eden," *Dictionary of the Pentateuch*, eds. T. Desmond Alexander and David W. Baker (Downers Grove: InterVarsity Press, 2003), 205. Walton stated, "When we see that creation as a whole was understood in terms of a cosmic temple complex, it would be logical to understand the garden as the antechamber to the holy of holies."

6. John Walton, *Genesis 1 as Ancient Cosmology* (Winona Lake: Eisenbrauns, 2011).

7. Dietrich Bonhoeffer, *Creation and Fall*, tr. John C. Fletcher (London: Collins, 1959), 70. Found in Victor Hamilton, *The Book of Genesis, Chapter 1–17*, New International Commentary on the Old Testament (Grand Rapids: Wm B. Eerdmans Publishing, 1990), 189.

8. John Steinbeck, *The Grapes of Wrath* (New York: Penguin Classics, 2006), 151.

CHAPTER 2

1. Washington Irving, *Washington Irving: A Treasury: Rip Van Winkle, The Legend of Sleepy Hollow, Old Christmas* (New York: Universe Publishing, 2012), 42–43.

2. Here we are referencing H. G. Wells's classic book *The Time Machine* and the film *Back to the Future*.

3. Stephen Hawking, "Essay 13: The Future of the Universe," *Black Holes and Baby Universes and Other Essays by Stephen Hawking* (New York: Bantam Books, 1993), 154.

4. Eugene Peterson, Lecture, Inverurie West Parish Church, Inverurie, Scotland, September 2009.

5. Victor Hamilton, *The Book of Genesis: Chapters 1–17*, New International Commentary on the Old Testament (Grand Rapids: Wm B. Eerdmans Publishing, 1990), 156. Hamilton stated, "The Hebrew uses assonance here: God formed ha adam . . . min ha adama. It is hard to capture this play on sounds in English, but it is something like 'God formed earthling from the earth.'"

6. John Calvin, *Calvin's Commentaries, Genesis*, vol. 1 (Grand Rapids: Baker Books, 2003), 111.

7. Karl Barth, *Church Dogmatics, The Doctrine of Creation*, vol. III.1, eds. Geoffrey W. Bromiley and Thomas Forsyth Torrance (Peabody: Hendrickson Publishing, 2010), 76–77.

8. It is, if nothing else, curious that when California shut down the 405 freeway for a weekend, the media linked this event to the apocalypse. The idea of traffic to that caliber, in the minds of many, might as well be the end of the world.

9. Neil Postman, *Amusing Ourselves to Death: Public Discourse in the Age of Show Business* (New York: Penguin Books, 1985), 11–12.

CHAPTER 3

1. Andy Crouch, "Steve Jobs: The Secular Prophet," *Wall Street Journal*, October 8, 2011, http://online.wsj.com/article/SB1000 14240529702034768045766154030281 27550.html.

CHAPTER 4

1. The material in this book about hiding and covering, stemming from the garden narrative, was first impressed upon us by our dear friend John Coe.

2. Our friend John Coe has developed this idea more deeply than anyone else we know.

3. In the words of our good friend John Coe.

CHAPTER 5

1. Karl Barth, *Church Dogmatics, The Doctrine of Reconciliations*, vol. IV.2, eds. Geoffrey W. Bromiley and Thomas Forsythe Torrance (Peabody: Hendrickson Publishing, 2010), 20–154.

This Christological reading of the parable derived from Karl Barth.

2. G. K. Beale, *The Temple and the Church's Mission: A Biblical Theology of the Dwelling Place of God*, New Studies in Biblical Theology (Downers Grove: InterVarsity Press, 2004), 95. I will be referencing Beale quite a bit in this short section. This book is truly masterful.

3. N. T. Wright, *Simply Jesus: A New Vision of Who He Was, What He Did, and Why He Matters* (New York: Harper One, 2011), 132–133.

4. Beale, *The Temple and the Church's Mission*, 62–63.

5. Wright, *Simply Jesus*, 133.

6. I have added in the implied "daughters" in this text.

7. I have added in the implied "daughters" in this text.

8. Graeme Goldsworthy, *Prayer and the Knowledge of God: What the Whole Bible Teaches* (Downers Grove: InterVarsity Press, 2003), 50.

CHAPTER 6

1. Hans Urs von Balthasar, *Prayer* (Ignatuis Press: Chicago, 1986), 133.

2. This conversation with Eugene Peterson took place at his home in Montana in 2012.

3. James W. Sire, *Praying the Psalms of Jesus* (Downers Grove: InterVarsity Press, 2007), 16.

4. Dietrich Bonhoeffer, *Life Together and Prayerbook of the Bible*, Dietrich Bonhoeffer Works, vol. 5, ed. Geffrey B. Kelly, trans. James H. Burtness (Minneapolis: Fortress Press, 1996).

5. Bonhoeffer, *Prayerbook of the Bible*, 156–57. One could also argue that the prayers of the Psalms were in fact Jesus' words prior to them being the words of the writers of the Psalms. As the eternal Word (John 1:1), Jesus was the source of every word of Scripture, via the Holy Spirit's inspiration. It is in this vein that Dietrich Bonhoeffer said, "Let us make no mistake: the Bible is God's Word, even in the Psalms. Then are the prayers

to God really God's own Word? That seems difficult for us to understand. We grasp it only when we consider that we can learn true prayer only from Jesus Christ, and that it is, therefore, the word of the Son of God, who lives with us human beings, to God the Father who lives in eternity."

6. John Calvin, *Calvin's Commentaries, Psalms 1–33*, vol. IV (Grand Rapids: Baker Books, 2003), xxxvii.

7. For further material on this, see R. T. France, *The Gospel of Mark*, New International Greek Testament Commentary (Grand Rapids: Wm B. Eerdmans Publishing, 2002), 581.

8. See Psalm 42:6 and Psalm 55:4–5 for Old Testament grounding in Jesus' statement.

9. Michael J. Gorman, *Cruciformity: Paul's Narrative Spirituality of the Cross* (Grand Rapids: Wm B. Eerdmans Publishing, 2001). We have found the word *cruciform* helpful in describing the nature of the Christian life.

10. Eugene Peterson, "Prayer," in *Dictionary for Theological Interpretation of the Bible*, ed. Kevin Vanhoozer (Grand Rapids: Baker Academic, 2005), 616.

11. Bonhoeffer, *Prayerbook of the Bible*, 156.

12. C. S. Lewis, *Reflections on the Psalms*, The Inspirational Writings of C. S. Lewis (New York: Inspirational Press, 1958), 134. C. S. Lewis added an interesting thought here when he said, "The Psalms are poems, and poems intended to be sung; not doctrinal treatise, nor even sermons."

CHAPTER 7

1. Michael Wilkens, *Matthew*, NIV Application Commentary (Grand Rapids: Zondervan, 2004), 275. Wilkens noted, "The motif of a 'heavenly Father' occurs throughout the Old Testament (e.g., Deut. 14:1; 32:6; Ps. 103:12; Hos. 11:1; Jer. 3:4; 31:9), growing increasingly popular during the Second Temple period in prayers for protection and forgiveness. Adult Jews often referred to God in prayer as 'our Father' (Heb. *'abuni*). The way Jesus uses '*my* Father' (11:27) to address his heavenly Father is

exceptional because Jesus is the unique Son (cf. 3:17). But by calling his disciples to share in the kingdom of heaven, they now have entered into a relationship with his Father as well."

2. N. T. Wright, "The Lord's Prayer as a Paradigm of Christian Prayer," in *Into God's Presence*, ed. Richard N. Longnecker (Grand Rapids: Wm B. Eerdmans Publishing, 2001), 132. Wright went on to state, "Seen with Christian hindsight—more specifically, with Trinitarian perspective—the Lord's Prayer becomes an invitation to share in the *divine life* itself. It becomes one of the high roads into the central mystery of Christian salvation and Christian existence: that the baptized and believing Christian is (1) incorporated into the inner life of the triune God *and* (2) intended not just to believe that this is the case, but actually to experience it."

3. Eugene Peterson, *Tell It Slant: A Conversation on the Language of Jesus in His Stories and Prayers* (Grand Rapids: Wm B. Eerdmans Publishing, 2008), 169.

4. Ibid.

5. Michael Wilkens, *Matthew*, 276.

6. Eugene Peterson, *Tell It Slant*, 186.

7. N. T. Wright, *Into God's Presence*, 147.

8. P. T. Forsyth, *The Soul of Prayer* (Vancouver: Regent College Publishing, 2002), 66.

9. John Calvin, *The Institutes of the Christian Religion*, ed. John T. McNeill (Louisville: Westminster John Knox Press, 1960), I, 1–2.

CHAPTER 8

1. G. K. Beale, *The Temple and the Church's Mission: A Biblical Theology of the Dwelling Place of God*, New Studies in Biblical Theology, ed. D. A. Carson (Downers Grove: InterVarsity Press, 2004), 313.

2. Ibid., 369.

3. Ibid., 370.

4. Ibid.

5. Ibid., 388.
6. Ibid., 389.
7. Ibid., 391.
8. This phrase is taken from the classic work on praying in the midst of the mundane, *The Practice of the Presence of God*, by Brother Lawrence.

CHAPTER 9

1. Jonathan Edwards, "Personal Narrative," in *Letters and Personal Writings*, The Works of Jonathan Edwards, vol. 16, ed. George S. Claghorn (New Haven: Yale University Press, 1998), 796.
2. Jonathan Edwards, "Discourse on the Trinity," in *Writings on the Trinity, Grace and Faith*, The Works of Jonathan Edwards, vol. 21, ed. Sang Hyun Lee (New Haven: Yale University Press, 2003), 173.
3. C. S. Lewis, *Letters to Malcolm Chiefly on Prayer: Reflections on the Dialogue Between Man and God* (New York: Harcourt, 1964), 68.
4. This idea of "sympathetic resonance" is from Jeremy Begbie, accessed October 19, 2012, http://www.youtube.com/watch?v=nQUetJuPeUs&feature=related.
5. I have added in the implied "daughters" in this text.
6. James Houston provided this phrase for us and has been a wonderful example of the "self-forgetfulness" the Lord calls us into.
7. François Fénelon, *Christian Classics: Meditations On the Heart of God*, trans. Robert J. Edmonson (Brewster: Paraclete Press, 1997), 124.

ABOUT THE AUTHORS //

PHOTOGRAPH BY JEREMY ELDER

JAMIN GOGGIN serves as Pastor of Spiritual Formation and Retreats at Saddleback Church. He holds an MA in Spiritual Formation and an MA in New Testament and is currently earning a PhD in Theology. He is the coeditor of *Reading the Christian Spiritual Classics: A Guide for Evangelicals.* Jamin speaks and writes from the depths of his own journey, seeking to invite others into the beauty and goodness of life with God. He lives with his wife and three children in Orange County, California.

//

KYLE STROBEL serves as an assistant professor of Spiritual Theology at Talbot School of Theology, Biola University, and speaks broadly on spiritual formation, theology, and the life of the church. Kyle holds a BA in Biblical Studies, master's degrees in Philosophy of Religion and Ethics as well as New Testament Studies, and a PhD in Systematic Theology. He is the author of several books, and his work is frequently published by periodicals such as *Relevant* magazine and Pastors.com. Driven to provide spiritual depth that is meaningful and yet accessible, Kyle writes and speaks from his own wrestling through prayer and life with God. He lives with his wife and two children in Fullerton, California.

METAMORPHA

Metamorpha Ministries is a spiritual formation ministry with a particular focus on articulating a distinctively evangelical understanding of the Christian life. Reaching back through our tradition to mine robustly Protestant and spiritual resources, Metamorpha seeks to proclaim the depths of the Gospel for a lived existence before the face of God. Our resources seek to be biblically, theologically, and spiritually informed, such that Christ never ceases to be the center.

In addition, Metamorpha.com is a ministry resource: for pastors, to help them live and lead in a healthy way in dependence upon Christ; for churches, to help them create communities of people growing in grace; and for individuals who are on a journey with Christ, to encourage, guide, and nurture an openness to the call of Christ on their lives.

FOR MORE INFORMATION, GO TO WWW.METAMORPHA.COM